MW00627676

All of the dramas on Earth
are nothing but a play
that is taking us to our awakening.

THE INTENDERS OF THE HIGHEST GOOD

The Ascenders Handbook

Two Roads Home

A Guide to
The Ascension Process

Tony Burroughs

Highest Light House

The Ascenders Handbook
Two Roads Home

Copyright © 2016 by Tony Burroughs

Printed in the United States of America

ISBN: 978-0-9819020-8-1

Dedicated to the Ascended Masters and Mentors
who came back - and to all who stand for the Highest Good

Published by:
Highest Light House
105 Highland Avenue
Pagosa Springs, CO 81147
Book Orders: 858-200-5200
info@highestlighthouse.com
www.highestlighthouse.com

For more information about
The Intenders of the Highest Good
visit www.intenders.com

For more information about the author
visit www.tonyburroughs.net

Table of Contents

The morning mist lifted leaving a crisp stillness in the air as the two men walked the narrow path through the ancient forest. "Is that the end of it?" asked the ever-curious Apprentice. "What about completing the octave? What about an 8th Ascension Reclamation?"

"You learn well, my young friend," replied the Master. "There is, most assuredly, an 8th Reclamation that completes the cycle. It's the one you'll claim for yourself... after you've experienced your Oneness and opted to come back and help others go where you have been."

Introduction

When *The Intenders Handbook* was first published, we were new to the skill of manifesting. We'd only been at it for a couple of years so there was much we still had to learn. Now, over twenty years later, we've fine-tuned these principles, added some new ones, built several models for coming together in community and greatly improved our proficiency in the field of deliberate manifestation.

The Ascenders Handbook: Two Roads Home, is an extension of *The Intenders Handbook,* sharing what we've learned since we founded the Intenders community. Written in the same style as our bestselling handbook, this sequel will familiarize you with the basic principles of two distinctly different roads you can travel to reach your highest fulfillment.

> ***You can manifest one thing***
> ***as easily as another -***
> ***if you believe that you can.***

In the first section, we'll explore the worldly road, the *Intention Process,* sharing stories from our own travels and experiences with the Intenders.

5

Then, we'll look at the major roadblocks and illusions that are keeping us from shining our highest light. In the final section, we'll present the *Ascension Process*, the inner road, for those who want to take a shortcut. If you're like us, having been brought up in the West with a whole slew of desires, you may want to do what we did: Follow one road for awhile, then follow the other and see where it takes you. Both roads lead to the same place, a place we call Home.

Home

You know what it's like when you come Home after a long trip. It feels good and there's no other place quite like it. It's not something you can adequately put into words. In fact, you don't want to analyze it too much because it's a feeling, and feelings tend to go away when we analyze them.

It's the same with our inner Home. It's a feeling, only this particular feeling is so good that we never want it to go away because it's better, *far better*, than any feeling we've ever had in our Earthly experience. That's the way it was for me the first time it happened in a remote bamboo forest in Kona. I'd never felt so good and I wanted more of it. Time went away, secrets were revealed, wrongdoing was dispelled and eternity opened up and showed me that my body would turn to dust one day, but that my Essence, the real me, goes on forever. It was, by far, the greatest experience of my life. Little did I realize that this sublime feeling would soon fade, and that I had a lot of work to do on myself in order to have it come back.

The nice thing I discovered along the way is that this feeling of Home is always deep inside me, in my heart and mind, even when I'm not aware of it. It can't go away. Even though I'm lost and alone on occasion, the feeling of Home is always there, resonating gently within me, awaiting my re-experience of it. And that's what the rest of this book is about: you, adventurous reader, and me, your humble scribe, moving together toward *an extraordinary experience* that's reaching out to us in the exact same measure that we reach out to it.

*Awakenings come in stages –
until we get to the Big Awakening.*

Two Roads

We've reached the point where we've manifested just about everything we intended. If it's been for the Highest Good, it's come to us, and if it wasn't for our Highest Good, we learned to do without it. Oh sure, there are some things we're likely to want in the future, but we've come to know that they'll be there for us when we intend for them.

That's where the *Intention Process* has taken us after having introduced it into our everyday lives over two decades ago. You see, in order for these ideas to have credibility, we have to have integrated them into our own lives. We need to have tested them and gotten proficient at manifesting before we could pass them along to you.

For me, personally, this integration has been the driving force throughout my entire adult life. In my travels to Intenders Circles across the country, people frequently ask what I've experienced as a result of having put the *Intention Process* to work in my own life. Do I have the material things I want? Am I happy? Am I spiritually awakened? In short, I'm a work in progress, just like you. I've found, though, that my focus has changed a bit over the years. Like most folks, I started out intending and manifesting worldly things: vehicles, places to live, money, relationships, success, etc. Nowadays, however, I'm more interested in the inner workings of my life, intending to know who I am at the core of my Being, intending to know God full-time.

What I've realized since I made these inner-directed intentions is that we have two time-tested roads we can follow to get to the feeling of Home: the *Intention Process* and the *Ascension Process*. Either road will take us there, and it is my intention in the following pages to travel each of these roads with you and point out some of the places of interest along the way. If it's okay with you, I'll bring my two mentors, BJ and Lee Ching, along for the ride to help us navigate the road Home easily and safely.

You're creating the world you're going to enter.

Briefly, the first road, the *Intention Process*, is one of fulfilling our worldly desires by making intentions. This is the road most people start out with, and I am no exception. Looking back, I've spent the better part of my life following this road and helping others get more proficient at manifesting their dreams and desires by using the *Intention Process*.

I recall one of our earliest Intenders Circles, just after we started having our 30 minute spiritual guidance sessions with Tina and Lee Ching. In it, I asked a question that all of us were interested in, namely "What about our desires? Are they good for us, or, as many of us have been taught, are they harmful? Will they keep us from reaching our highest fulfillment?"

The answer we received was both surprising and profound. Lee Ching told us that we're born with our desires; that we come into this lifetime with them, and that it's our calling to either transcend or fulfill these desires until we get to the point where there aren't any of them anymore. This, he said, was what the Buddhist teachings call reaching the state of "desirelessness". He told us that different cultures tend to treat their desires differently. In the East, where spirituality is more in the forefront of their lifestyle, people are more apt to pray and meditate in order to transcend their desires. He went on to say that the Buddhists believe that all of our suffering comes from our attachment to the things of this world and that we can achieve inner peace and rise up and out of our suffering by ridding ourselves of

10

our desires through prayer, meditation and right action.

"It's different in the West," he said. "Inner pursuits play a much smaller role in America than they do in other parts of the world. You tend to be more materially oriented here, wanting to amass great wealth in the form of money and possessions." At this point Lee Ching emphasized that there is absolutely nothing wrong with this proclivity of our Western culture; it's just that it lends itself to a different approach for those who would seek a higher experience. He said that the fulfillment of our desires is a bona fide road Home. We can learn to "Knock them off, one at a time, until they're gone." In this way, he said, we reach the same state of desirelessness that the seekers in the East reach.

Well, this was music to my ears. Like most folks in America, I had loads of desires. What with the constant bombardment of advertising from the mainstream media, we'd all been programmed to want all sorts of things. From our earliest childhood, we were taught to have a myriad of desires; it's just that nowhere in our schooling were we taught how to get good at fulfilling them. In fact, most people, myself included, didn't have a clue about getting proficient at manifesting - and, as a result, most of us wanted more fulfillment, but didn't know how to get it by any means other than working

11

hard and going into long-term debt. We had no idea that our thinking had anything to do with our future; that, instead of working so hard, we could "think things into existence" by making deliberate, conscious intentions.

As I glanced across the table at Mark, Tina and Betsy (my fellow cofounders of The Intenders), we all had the same look in our eyes, the same resonant feeling inside. It was like a light bulb went off in all of us at the same time. We could learn to fulfill our desires by making intentions. What a great idea! What if we sat in a circle, shared our intentions and envisioned everyone else's intentions manifesting, as well? Wouldn't that accelerate everything?

Looking back, it was the guidance from Lee Ching that evening that sparked us into starting our Intenders community. Little did we realize at the time that we were creating a model for people all over the world to fulfill their desires by sitting in a weekly circle with their friends and sharing their intentions. We never dreamed it would turn out to be as popular as it is.

Or did we?

The second road Home is what we call the *Ascension Process*. This inner road takes up where the worldly road leaves off, offering us a shortcut on our journey by helping us change the way we perceive things. In other words, we can learn to see things differently, and we can begin by making some basic changes in our everyday behavior. For openers, we can learn to retain our peace of mind and remain unaffected by external worldly circumstances. We can practice being positive and happy, regardless of what's going on in our outer, material world.

One beautiful Hawaiian morning I was seeking some clear direction about money and how was I supposed to be happy with all the bills constantly coming in? In those days I owned a 4.5 acre avocado farm on the Kona Coast of the Big Island, and the expenses of this project weighed heavily on me from time to time. I had come to Kona to get out of the rat race, raise my own food and live more in nature. But I hadn't figured in the cost of all this.

When I arrived at his little coffee shack that morning, my first mentor, BJ, was having his usual eggs and toast as he sat overlooking the entire southwestern coastline. After chatting a few moments, I asked him about my money issues. I didn't realize at the time that the answer he gave was to have a much greater effect on the rest of my life than I ever would've expected. He said that we have a couple of options when it comes to dealing with money and the monthly bills. The first option was to go out and do whatever is necessary to make a million dollars. He told me that this will likely take a few years out of my life, and then, after I'd accumulated enough money in this way, I could use it to create the kind of environment I wanted for myself.

The second option, he said, was to be deliberately poor, to live life as it comes, and trust that everything I needed would be there for me when I need it. He went on to say that if I looked back on my life I would find that whatever I needed, not just for my survival, but also for my creative projects, had always been there for me. The Universe was user friendly, he said, and that all I had to do to take advantage of this "user friendliness" was to believe in it and stop sabotaging myself with my all-too-frequent scarcity rants.

I started to react with one of the rants he was referring to, but he quickly interrupted. "By the way," he said, "there's another big plus that comes with choosing the path of deliberate poverty: it can begin immediately, right in this very moment. You won't have to go anywhere or go through any of the challenges that are demanded of those who choose the millionaire route. You can be happy, money-wise, right now as we sit overlooking this amazing Pacific Ocean, knowing that somehow, unbeknownst to you, your needs will always be taken care of."

I sat there mulling this over as he poured more coffee for both of us. I'd never thought about my life like this before. Here was true insight! But it would take trust. Big trust! As if to know what I was thinking, he added, "Tony, you can make a million dollars or you can be poor on purpose. In terms of money, either one will lead you to your freedom. Anything in between leads to middle class servitude and tends to encumber you in a very short time. I don't think that is what you want for yourself..."

As you may have guessed, I chose the second option and the benefits started rolling in right away. I was able to stay on the farm full-time, and I was free to get up every morning and do what I wanted to do each day. I didn't have to go to work or sell out to anyone or compromise my values. Sure, there were times when things were a bit tight financially, and I had to take on temporary odd jobs pruning trees or landscaping for the neighbors. But these were fun, and as long as I trusted and remembered that my happiness is in my mind and that it didn't have to be affected by the amount of money in my wallet or my bank account, everything always managed to work out fine.

Your challenges are never outside of you.
Your challenges are always inside of you.

While the *Intention Process* is for people who want to get good at fulfilling their worldly desires by making intentions, the *Ascension Process* is for those who are beginning to look inward. It's about having *an extraordinary inner experience*, sometimes called the Atonement, Unity, The Holy Instant or Oneness. We'll talk more about that later. For now, let's turn our attention back to the first road, to getting good at manifesting what we want.

Remember!
All roads take you Home.
You cannot fail to get there.
It's just a matter of how long it takes.

Part 1
The Intention Process Revisited
Fulfilling Our Worldly Desires

People wonder why we've had such great success manifesting the things we've intended, and the answer is simple. We follow the *Intention Process*. In other words, we do three things that are enhancing our manifesting skills exponentially: 1) We say our intentions (or prayers or affirmations) every morning; 2) We get together in a circle with like-minded and light-hearted friends every week or two and share our gratitudes and intentions; 3) And we always line our intentions up with the Highest Good by saying that in order for them to manifest they must serve the Highest Good of the Universe, ourself and everyone everywhere.

Hi. My name is Lara and my girlfriend and I are starting an Intenders Circle here in Calgary, Alberta, Canada. I just wanted to relay a story that happened while I was in the middle of reading "The Code". I locked my keys in my car at the grocery store and I didn't have a spare or money for a locksmith, so I decided

I'd try making an intention - so I said 'I intend to find a locksmith and he's going to open my car for free!"

I did my shopping, got a hanger, and on my way out of the store a guy noticed the hanger and asked if I locked my keys in my car. I told him yes, and he said "Well, what kind of car is it?" So I told him and he said "Man, those are hard to break into." I remember thinking, "God, I said a locksmith, not a car thief!"

To make a long story short, he tried to get into my car, but couldn't. After about 10 minutes he told me he'd be right back. He came back with his locksmith kit and opened my car for free. Thank you so much for the gift you're sharing with the world. I'm intending that the new Calgary Intenders will start to manifest their intentions like never before.

Lara Huget

Intenders Circle Updates

Since we made our first Intenders DVD showing how we run an Intenders Circle, we've added a couple of things that have caught on in all the circles we've visited. As you know, when it's our turn to share in the circle, we first say our gratitudes for the things we're grateful for in our lives (including the manifestation of intentions we made in previous circles.) Then, we say our intentions for the things that we want or need. These can be anything from intending for a new car to intending for inner peace. We can intend anything we like, as long as we line it up with the Highest Good.

I've seen so many beautiful manifestations happen as a result of people making intentions in our Intenders Circles. Here's just one example. My old Dodge van was getting tired, and I needed a newer one so I could get around the country to do my work. I was in Redding, CA in an Intenders Circle and made an intention that I have a newer, more reliable, custom, conversion van with all the bells and whistles. The next day, my old van went into the shop for another minor repair and, there, on the counter, as I was paying my bill for the repair, was a flyer for a beautiful newer Dodge conversion van. I tore off one of the phone number tags and called the lady who happened to live 3 blocks from the repair shop. In 10 minutes I was looking at one of the fanciest vans I'd ever seen. There was only one problem, though. I didn't have the $12,000 she wanted for it. I didn't even have a thousand dollars at the time because I'd just spent everything I had to get on tour.

The following day I was in another Intenders Circle in the next town, Grants Pass, Oregon. When it came my turn to make my intentions, I stated the same intention I made in the Redding Intenders Circle: that I have a newer, wonderful conversion van and that it comes to me freely, easily and effortlessly.

Right after the circle, I was standing outside the yoga studio where we had gathered, and a man from the circle approached me. He said his name was Pete and that he just inherited a great deal of money, and that he would gladly buy me a van! I cannot tell you how good it felt! I immediately called the lady in Redding back and made all the arrangements. A few days later, I was back in Redding, driving away in my newer, and much fancier, Dodge conversion van . . . all because of an amazingly generous man I'd never even met before. Thank God for the power of the Intenders Circle!

Tony Burroughs

There is magic in your Intenders Circles. You make good friends, manifest your desires, and keep each other awake to what you're creating with your thoughts and words.

Our first new addition to the Intenders Circle happens when an Intender finishes saying his or her intentions. At this point we integrated the Ninth Intent of *The Code* by sharing our visions for our ideal world. It works like this: after we say our gratitudes and intentions, we would also share a vision for a better world by saying, *"I see a world where...."* It could be anything that you think will make this world a better place, such as: *"I see a world where every child born on this Earth is loved, nurtured, cared for and honored by every other person who lives on this planet. And that all living beings - humans and animals alike - are allowed to live out their natural lives to full completion without them being interrupted or interfered with by anyone else who lives here."*

We do this because, over the years, we've learned that when we share our vision for our ideal world, we're consciously contributing to the creation of it. Intenders love this part of the sharing because it makes them feel like they're truly making a difference in our world - and they are!

It started with a dream that woke me at 3 am. In it, I was guided to create a website, call it the Vision Alignment Project, and write short Visions about my ideal world on every subject from the better treatment of the dolphins to bringing the Highest Good into the business arena. Then, I was to email the Visions out twice a week for free to our subscribers. The dream also guided me to place a big green "YES I Align with this Vision" Button after each Vision and connect it to a hit counter. This way, when people clicked the big green button, it would show them exactly how many others have aligned with my Visions. In addition, I was also shown that whenever someone clicked the YES Button, they would be actively contributing to the manifestation of that Vision. In short, it would be a great way for people who didn't otherwise know how they could make a difference in our world to do so.

As of this printing, more than 400 Visions have been penned by myself and people from all over the world - and our subscribers have hit the big green YES button more than 2 million times! Needless to say, we are amazed by the success of this one-of-a-kind project. It shows us that people truly want a world that is more supportive - and they believe they can have it!

You can sign up for the VAP at
www.visionalignmentproject.com.

Can you imagine what it will be like
when we all care for each other;
when everyone is helping everyone else;
when everyone has whatever they need.

Angel Wings and Oneness

We've also added another step to our Intention Circles. In the past, each person would finish up their turn in the circle by saying, "Do you Align with me?" or "Are you with me?" – and everyone else would chime in, saying "YES!" Then, he or she would say, "So be it!" and everyone else would say, "And so it is!" in unison.

Here is where we added something new. After everyone says, "And so it is," the Intender now says, "It is done. It is done. It is done!" – and that's not all! Awhile back, the Intenders in San Diego started waving their "angel wings" while saying "It is done", and it was so much fun that we do it in every circle nowadays.

Here's how it works: as everyone in the circle is saying "It is done" 3 times in unison, they're also waving their angel wings by interlocking their thumbs and wiggling their fingers toward the person who is just finishing their turn. It sounds silly, but it feels so good that everyone wants to do it. You can see these new additions, including the angel wings, on our Intenders Cybercircles videos on The Intenders YouTube Channel.

As those of you who have been in our circles know, creating the experience of Oneness has always been built into our gatherings. We're setting the stage several times throughout the evening for Oneness to occur by toning together (at the end of the meeting) and by chiming in together in unison every time we say "YES" and "So be it" and "It is done!" Each time we all say these things at the same time, we're moving ourselves that much closer to the Atonement (At-One-Ment).

Now you know why people have such a great time in our Intenders Circles. It's because it feels so wonderful when we do things as One.

Whenever people meet together,
they can set the stage for the Atonement.
Then they will remember who they really are.

Sharing

Sharing is a wonderful thing at certain times and not such a good idea at other times. When we share our intentions in an Intenders Circle, it serves us greatly because these intentions are lined up with the Highest Good. Indeed, we always feel free to share our intentions with others who are likeminded and lined up with the Highest Good. In this way, our intentions will manifest more readily because our friends in the circle are seeing them manifest along with us. It's a "strength in numbers" factor. The more people you can get to align with your intentions, the quicker and easier they will manifest for you.

Likewise, we also share intentions in our circles on behalf of other people. In fact, people frequently ask us whether it's okay to make intentions for others, such as their ill family members or their friends in need - and the answer is positively Yes! It's fine to make intentions for others, as long as the Highest Good is in play. By the same token, we do not recommend that intentions are made for others when the Highest Good is not mentioned. We wouldn't want to be controlling or manipulative in the lives of others, and, unless the Highest Good is invoked, that's exactly what would happen. In short, the Highest Good clause sees to it that our intentions are loving and are not interfering with the journeys of our friends and family.

You can make intentions for others as long as you line them up with the Highest Good.

Now let's look at sharing from a slightly different point of view. There are times when all of us have been in conversations where someone is talking at length about their challenges. Perhaps they're sick or broke or recently separated from a loved one. In these instances, we feel compassion for them, but we do not agree with them about these issues because, if we did, we'd be reinforcing them. We'd be helping them advance their own suffering.

By the same token, we refrain from sharing the details of our own challenges for the same reason: we'd be reinforcing them. You see, when we talk about the challenges we're experiencing in our lives, we're making them stronger. It's the same principle that works for us in a positive way in our Intenders Circles. When we get someone else to line up with whatever we're sharing, it makes it bigger, more apt to manifest. So we've found that it's wise to be discerning about what we're sharing. If we're sharing about something that serves us and our fellow travelers, then this is a good idea, and it will bring us the results we're looking for. However, when we're sharing about the difficulties in our lives, we're making them stronger, as well, and we're unlikely to get the results we're looking for.

Of course, when we need help, it's wise to tell another person what's going on in our life. But there's a point where asking for help can easily turn into wallowing in our dramas, and this is not advisable. Asking for help and going into too much detail are two different animals. Seeking help from our friends leads to healing, while over-dramatizing our situation leads to more suffering, especially when we give names to our challenges. That's why we don't mention the names of sicknesses and diseases in our Intenders Circles: because it makes them stronger. It reinforces the sickness instead of the wellness, and it doesn't help anyone.

Lee Ching told us long ago that whatever we're talking about, whether it's positive or

27

negative, is working its way into the forefront of our future. And yet, it's extremely common in today's world to hear folks adding to their difficulties by dwelling at length on the negative. Isn't it time we took a closer look at this strange habit? Isn't it time we became a bit more vigilant of what we're creating with our everyday thoughts and words?

When someone is going on about their drama, you can suggest that they make an intention around it - and very soon, the drama will be gone because the intention they made has manifested for them.

Creating or Miscreating?

Did you ever say something and immediately wish you hadn't said it? Doesn't feel so good, does it? This is because part of you knew that you'd just set the wheels in motion for all sorts of crazy experiences to come your way - all because you didn't stop yourself. By the same token, did you ever start to say something that you didn't want to be manifesting in a million years, and you caught yourself before you said it? Felt good, even though it seemed like you were going to burst inside, didn't

28

it? Now you won't have to go through all those crazy situations that you would have had to deal with if you had opened your mouth at that moment.

This scenario happens all the time. We're suddenly faced with a point in our conversations where we can feel that it's our turn to talk in order to keep the momentum of the conversation going. Everybody's looking at us, waiting to hear what we have to say - and it's at this point where we have a snap decision to make. We can agree or disagree or be silent. Depending on which choice we make, it can take us closer to or farther away from our happiness. So, our decision rests upon whether what we're about to say will serve us and our friends, or not. If we say something that doesn't serve us, we'll have to pay the price. But if we catch ourself before saying anything, we can change the direction of the entire rest of our life.

I had this happen to me at a party recently. I was sitting on a large circular couch with a bunch of friends and a couple of strangers. One of the strangers, whose name was Millie, was talking about how she hated getting older. She droned on well past the point of comfortable conversation. She complained about her legs, her back, her neck. She complained about her lack of finances, her lack of family, her lack of friends. She complained about the government and the healthcare system, and just as her complaints were reaching their crescendo, she turned to me and said, "What do you think about getting older, Tony?

Well, to be honest, there was a part of me who was primed and ready to commiserate with her. I even heard a voice in my head say something I had said without thinking in similar situations in the past. But this time I caught myself - and I stopped for a moment, just long enough to ask myself if saying anything would serve me, or her, or anyone else on the couch. The answer I got was clear. If I agreed with her about her complaints about aging, I would be setting myself (and everyone else who was listening) up to experience the very same things she was experiencing. On the other hand, if I withheld my agreement, it would keep us all of us out of harm's way. So finally, after several seconds, I looked straight at her and said, "Hmmm, Millie, what you say is interesting...but it hasn't been my experience."

Driving home from the party that night, I was mulling over that conversation and breathed a huge sigh of relief. I'd caught myself just in time. If I would have agreed with her...well, let's not even go there.

You don't have to agree with everybody about everything.

Here's something you can do right away that is both fun and uplifting at the same time: *start watching your words.* Begin by objectively observing what you're saying both to yourself and to others. You'll be amazed at what you find yourself creating with your everyday thoughts and words because, when you begin to watch even closer, you'll soon discover that, in many instances, you're saying things that won't lead you anywhere near your happiness, your joy or your goals in life. In far too many instances we're sabotaging ourselves by thinking and saying things that we wouldn't ever want to manifest. This can be a little disconcerting for some people when they first start out.

So ... we suggest that you stay lighthearted when you're watching your words because, when you do, there's something else that happens that will benefit you, as well. You'll open yourself to receive a reward much greater than you might have anticipated. Indeed, every time we catch ourself (and it may even be in mid-sentence) before saying something unserving, and we say something more

31

positive instead, we raise our consciousness - and everything in our life will proceed differently from that moment on.

As most of you know, I live on the Big Island of Hawaii where we started the Intenders. Last month the people who rent the downstairs area of my house had to move suddenly, so I was thinking about how to get some new renters to come in. A few days went by and one night I woke up in the middle of the night worrying about having the empty space and no income from the rental. I remember my ego's thoughts vividly, "What am I going to do NOW?" and "I have to do something!!" I was starting to feel afraid - you know what I'm talking about . . .

Then, all of a sudden, I caught myself and decided to start meditating. I went into that Higher Self space that I go to when I'm channeling, made an intention around having new renters, and instantly my fears went away. I heard my Higher Self say, "You're going to be okay," and I felt wrapped in love, totally taken care of, knowing there is nothing whatsoever to be concerned about.

Two days later, a lady named Eleanor called from the mainland. She had heard Tony on a blog-talk radio show and was thinking that the Intenders was just what she needed. She looked up the Intenders website and saw me there and read the story about how we started the original Intenders Circle. "Is there still an Intenders Circle on the Big Island," she asked. When I said yes she said, "Mike, my husband, and I are thinking about moving to Hawaii. Do you know of any places to live near you?" I told her that I had an empty apartment downstairs from me - and the next thing she said was, "We'll take it!"

That was about a month ago. They're all moved in now and they love it here! And, as for me, I couldn't have asked for better people to be my new neighbors.

Tina Stober

*In times of no money,
you still have your intentions.
You can still manifest whatever you need
by intending it.*

Our Thoughts Are Causing It All

Is what we're thinking going to give us the results we're intending for? This is the question we can be asking ourselves throughout the day, especially when we're dealing with negative thoughts, thoughts that clearly aren't pointing us in the direction we want to go. Holding our attention on positive outcomes is the best thing we can do. Why would anyone want to continue to hold fast to a negative thought once they recognize the effect it's going to have on them and those around them?

No matter how we look at it, our thoughts are the causes, and our experiences are the effects. This is true in all circumstances regardless of whether we're aware of it or not. We can't have an outcome without a thought that caused it. Unfortunately, people nowadays are spending huge amounts of time and energy sifting through their effects in order to resolve their issues, when the resolution lies in the cause, in the thought that first gave rise to the situation they're in. In other words, they're looking in the wrong place. It's like trying to catch a fish on dry land. If we want to fix something that's not working for us, we have to seek out the thoughts that caused our challenges in the first place.

Our healthcare system is riddled with miscreation. It entirely discounts our thinking processes and has us believing that we can get well by treating the symptoms and the effects of our suffering. BJ used to get all riled up when the subject of sickness arose. "I can't believe that people keep buying into the mainstream medical mindset," he said one day as we were taking a break from building an addition onto his small coffee shack. "We'll never get out of the medical dark ages as long as we continue to rely on pills and devices to make us well. These things only treat the symptoms and not the true cause."

"What are you talking about, BJ," I asked. I was raised in a medical family - my dad was a doctor and my mom was a nurse - and I was brought up to believe that we get well by following the doctor's advice.

"It's all about bucks," he said. "The doctors do what the pharmaceutical salespeople tell them to do, and the bottom line for the pharmaceutical companies is profits, not healing people."

What he was saying took me back to my childhood. I remember all-too-many instances when my dad told me to come down to his office after school because the "detail man" - that's what he called the pharmaceutical salesman - had brought in a new vaccine he wanted to try out on me. From my point of view, there was nothing wrong with me. I was fine, and I surely didn't need to be injected with any substances I didn't know anything about. Some of those concoctions hurt my young body, but I didn't have a choice. He was my dad, and I was a child who trusted him to have my best

35

interests at heart.

BJ knew what I was thinking. "They only treat the effects with their pills and vaccinations," he said, "and they never treat the true cause, which is in the mind. You see, Tony, nothing just happens to us, like the medical people would have us believe. Sicknesses don't come from out of nowhere. They happen in the mind first because we've been taught how to get sick by the medical people themselves. I know it's hard for those of us who really care about one another to believe that the pharmaceutical companies would consciously create diseases so they can sell their pills and potions to make big money, but you don't have to watch TV for very long to see that this is true. They're selling every kind of sickness imaginable - sicknesses and diseases that they've created in their own think tanks and laboratories. They hire people with no conscience to invent and advertise their diseases, and they don't care about healing people at all. In fact, it's just the opposite. They want people to get sick so they can make more money. It's as simple as that!"

I was lost in thought as his rant wound down and his voice took on a softer tone. "Tony, a true healer doesn't tell people how sick they are or make questionable diagnoses. He knows that most people are suggestible and that they easily believe and manifest what they are told, especially when it comes from an authority figure.

A true healer knows that all healing happens first in the mind, and so he sees the people who come to him as already well. He holds the light for others; he doesn't send them spinning off into darkness by reinforcing their sickness. And he surely doesn't prescribe devices like pills and potions, unless that's the only thing the patient believes will bring relief. A true healer knows that, somewhere in the back of the patient's mind, he or she bought into the suggestion of sickness, and thus created it.

The healer's job is to help the patient replace that thought of sickness, which was originated by the medical media, with the thought of perfect health. How can the patient ever get well as long as he thinks he is sick? Since it all started in his mind, he has to think he is well, regardless of whatever is going on in his body. This is what we'll be rediscovering someday, just as soon as we come out of the medical dark ages."

Of course, the healthcare system is only one example of how we sabotage ourselves by clinging to thoughts that aren't serving us. The same could easily be said for any ideas we have where we're giving our power over to others who say they care about us, but really don't. It's time for us to take our personal power back by realizing that we're doing it all to ourself; that it is we who make the decision to allow others to invade our thinking - and it is we who can choose, at any moment, to think whatever we want. There's no one standing over us with a bullwhip telling us what to think. We can think what we want, and thus, we can create what we want.

The key to manifesting a happy, fulfilled life:
Envision Only Positive Outcomes.

The Highest Good

As *The Intenders Handbook* was becoming popular, I came to the mainland from Hawaii and began traveling around the country showing people how we conduct our Intenders Circles. People from all walks of life wanted to know just what was causing us to have such great success manifesting our intentions. When I first started out, I found that I was spending most of my time in front of the groups explaining the fine points of intention making - and as a result, many of the people I was talking to started up Intenders Circles of their own. This is how the Intenders spread so rapidly across the country. I felt like an ambassador for intentionality.

Then, after a couple of years, something changed. After witnessing how the Highest Good was working so beautifully, not only in my own life, but in the lives of Intenders I was meeting from Seattle to Miami, I realized that It was playing a much greater part in our Intention Circles than I previously thought. Of course, I continued to be an ambassador for intention-making after that, but as I kept witnessing the wondrous effects of the Highest Good, I began emphasizing It even more in my presentations. It was at this point when I noticed I was not just an ambassador for intentionality. I'd also become an ambassador for the Highest Good.

Just as the spokes of a wheel are held together by a hub, so are the Intenders held together by the Highest Good. The Highest Good is the focal point that everything else in the Intenders revolves around. Without it, we would just be another manifesting group. But with it, we insure that everything we intend and manifest is covered by the Highest Good. What do we mean by that? It means that whatever we're creating in our lives serves the Highest Good. How do we do it? We add the following phrase at the end of all our intentions: *"in order for these intentions to manifest, they must serve the Highest and Best Good of the Universe, myself, and everyone everywhere."* Since we've learned that *what we say is what we get*, we know that, by saying this simple phrase, we're lining our intentions, as well as our lives, up with the Highest Good.

By the same token, we've discovered that when we add this phrase at the end of our intentions, if something isn't manifesting for us, then it's not for our Highest Good. In this way, the Highest Good is like a safety net. If our intent is for the Highest Good, it will manifest, and if it's not for our Highest Good, it won't.

When I found the Highest Good, it was like something in my life clicked into place. I'd made intentions before and manifested a few things, but something wasn't quite right. I kept getting things that didn't quite work out for me. The shoes that manifested were the wrong size, the car that manifested needed major repairs, the relationship that manifested went sour right away, and so on. I couldn't figure out why these things were happening until I ran across the concept of the Highest Good. Right off the bat, it resonated with me... I started saying the Highest Good clause at the end of my intentions and it wasn't long before I had new shoes that fit like a glove, the car miraculously fixed itself, and a new lady, who is one of the sweetest people I've ever met, came into my life. It was like I had the magic touch. But, looking back, I can see that it wasn't magic at all. It was the Highest Good!   *Rob Eastman*

**When you are always asking
for the highest and best good,
that is all that can be delivered to you.**

Manifesting for Free.
Are You Kidding Me ?

Hi Tony, I have been meaning to write to you to tell you how very grateful I am to you, and all of the Intenders. Today I was talking to a friend on the phone, and I mentioned "The Code" and how important its been in my life. I bought your book, "Get What You Want" over a year ago, and have read it twice and I use it daily to find comfort and guidance. It has helped me with so many miracles. She did not know anything about "The Intenders", so I told her my story.

I feel that I am a Mighty Manifester most of the time — I do slip a little — so let me tell you about the biggest miracle that intending brought to me.

I got the idea from your book because there was a woman who intended a home for herself freely and easily — and I thought — I can do that. Without going into a long story, I lost my beautiful home and studio in Phoenix about three years ago. I then stayed at my sister's house in Marshfield, Massachusetts. She is the one that got me started in "Intending" and I stayed there for almost two years. From there, I rented a cottage on the ocean for six months in the middle of the worst

*winter ever in New England to get myself together...
and this is where I started intending a new home for
myself. I was homeless — okay — high end homeless,
yet nonetheless, it is not a great place to be.*

*Here is what I wrote: "I intend that I am creating a
home with a studio that is light and airy and peaceful.
The home is large and beautiful and is in a quiet
neighborhood, and I have a magical place to paint. This
home comes to me freely and easily. For the highest good
of all concerned. So be it, and so it is."*

*I read my intention just about every day — and
thought about it, smiled, and let it go. When the thought
came up about "freely" — are you kidding me, Diane,
well, I just let it go. Two months went by, and just as
I was about to leave the cottage in May, my second-
cousin, once removed, Fred (who is eighty) called to ask
me if I would like to stay in his home in Ocala, Florida.
He was building a home with his new woman, Jean, and
he told me that he was laying in bed and thought of me
and decided to offer me his house — for free! All I had
to do was to pay the utilities.*

*Needless to say, I was blown away — I couldn't believe
it — I truly was incredibly grateful to the Universe! I
danced around all day, still in somewhat of a "cloud."
That night I was going to a dinner party with my sister,*

43

Maryanne, and her husband, Marty, and I told them the story in the car on the drive over to the party. By the time we got to the party, the energy was so amazing. All of the people at the party were from a group that gathered every week and we read spiritual and loving books, and to start the evening we read our Intentions, so you can imagine how they related to my "intention"!

Well, I arrived in late January when their new home was finally ready — and, here I am. Did I mention that this house also has a pool? And, the master bathroom is bigger than the bedroom that I spent several months in. When I arrived here, it seemed like it was full of "instant manifestations", as it is fully furnished with everything, including laundry products, pots and pans, dishes, etc. The house is huge and I have set up my painting studio in the main room right off the kitchen. I love it here. It is a new adventure and I am excited and very grateful for this amazing place to live.

Diane Leonard
www.dianeleonard.com

The Highest Good has the most beautiful plans for both you and the world. You just have to open up to it.

Part II
Removing the Roadblocks

Overcoming Doubts and Limitations

In our work with the Intenders over the years, we've noticed a distinct pattern emerge. Once we've gotten good at intending and manifesting our worldly desires, we typically move on to working with our inner attributes, intending for more peace, more patience, more courage, and so forth. For most folks, this is the first step on the path of Ascension, or Atonement. We fine-tune our positive traits. We hone our character. We seek connection with our Essence.

Our Essence, or Spirit, is who we really are, and it's not until we transcend the body and live from our Essence that we no longer experience pain and suffering. The nice thing about this is that our Essence is always right there with us. We needn't go anywhere in order to find It. All we need to do is uncover the blocks between us and It.

Every positive thought serves you.
Every negative thought sabotages you.

At almost every Intenders event someone raises a question about doubts. From our point of view, doubting is the opposite direction from where we want to go. It's a limitation or a resistance, like a roadblock crossing our path, keeping us from having the outcomes we're intending for. And, like all limitations, the more attention we put on it, the bigger it gets.

Rarely a day goes by without us running across someone who is deep in a drama and arguing on behalf of their limitations. Typically, they're holding fast to the idea that they can't have what they want. When this happens we usually point out what they're doing to themself, and we can tell right away whether they're going to become a Mighty Manifester or not by how firm they're holding on to their limiting ideas.

I have a buddy named Michael who really wants to be in a loving relationship, but it just hasn't manifested for him in the several years I've known him. Michael is a very good looking, outgoing, friendly guy and there is no reason in the world why he couldn't be in a relationship - except for one: when you ask him about what he's doing in order to find the woman of his dreams, he'll immediately go into all the reasons why it's not happening. He'll say he's not handsome enough, he's not financially set, he's too old, he's too independent, he's lives too far out in the country, etc. And here's his latest limiter: he says that even if he found the right woman, he doesn't trust himself to be good enough for her, or good enough to her. He thinks she'd leave right away, or he would. Yikes! I want to cringe! My good friend is about as stubborn as it gets! The more I point out that he's arguing heavily on behalf of all the things that are keeping him from enjoying the relationship he so badly desires, the more he comes up with new ways to sabotage himself.

Isn't it interesting how we tend to keep the things we want most at bay by thinking we can't have them? Lee Ching used to help us with this by using an old cliché in an amusing sort of way. When one of us started to bring out our "poor me" in one way or another, he'd smile and say, "You know what happens when you argue for your limitations, don't you? You get to keep them."

Two months ago Michael and I were having breakfast at our local coffee shop, and he was going through his recurring story about wanting to be in relationship and all the reasons why it's not happening. So I told him

47

exactly what Lee Ching told us. When I smiled and said, "You get to keep them," he shut up. I could see the wheels going round in his head. He was starting to realize what he was doing to himself.

Since that day I haven't seen as much of Michael. He found himself a pretty country girl and he's out at her place most of the time. The last time I saw him he had that sweet, shiny look of love in his eyes. I can't tell you how happy I am for him - not just because he's in a loving relationship now, but also because he's not arguing for his limitations anymore.

You get whatever you put your attention on.

The Blame Game

Our ego is the consummate trickster. It's deceiving us every step of the way, telling us that we're better than, prettier than, richer than, more deserving than, even happier than those around us. There's only one problem with this: our ego's words are all lies. Like the snake in the Garden of Eden, it's doing everything it can to keep us away from knowing the truth about who we really are and what is really going on here in this Earthly realm and beyond.

One of the ego's favorite tricks is the blame game, where we're constantly looking outside ourself for someone to blame for whatever's bothering us. We set ourselves up to become victims by denying any responsibility for being the cause of own experiences. We say *"She did it to me; I am not responsible here!"* - all the while forgetting that we had something to do with what happened. We made the decision to be there in the first place.

Deep within us, we know we are causing our own experiences. Here on Earth, however, we play the blame game because it gets us attention, or it brings us money, or validation for our actions, or the feeling of superiority, or an excuse to run off our excess emotional charge on others. In short, we have *a vested interest* in our victimhood; we're getting something out of it. But that "something" pales in comparison to what we could be experiencing if we stopped playing the game.

I've played the blame game most of my life. Not until recently did I realize how much it was keeping me from my true happiness. Like many folks out there, my favorite thing to blame was the government. They were overtaxing me, spraying me with aerial poisons, lying about what's in my foods, creating false enemies, instigating wars and lying about it, acting solely on behalf of big business, taking the money out of the hands of the average person and filling the pockets of those who already have plenty, forcing me to have insurance I don't want or need, and on and on. They taught me in school that they were going to represent me; that we are a government "of the people, for the people and by the people." But that is clearly no longer the case.

The more I thought about all their shenanigans, the angrier I got. If they were trying to upset me, they were doing a good job of it. It looked like my only way out was to resign myself to putting up with their tricks and being unhappy about it. My back was against the wall. What could I do?

It was about that time that Lee Ching taught me about the boogieman. After listening so supportively to my complaints about the government, he began by saying that the lawmakers of today are the lawbreakers of today, and that governments are always moving toward dictatorship. Then, as he always does, he veered to the positive side, saying, "Tony, the awakened person acts while the unawakened person reacts. Reacting goes nowhere. Continue to fight with the boogieman and you're reacting. You don't need to react to what seems to be going on out there. If everyone would just stop reacting and tune in to what their true purpose is, to what they're doing here, everything would clear up politically, economically, and personally in a jiffy."

As I was flashing on this, he told me one more thing that set me off in the right direction. "In the midst of all the strife and craziness, millions are waking up to the realization that we are all One," he said, and, from that moment on, I let go of being a victim to the whims of the government and remembered my true purpose. I remembered that I could be happy in the midst of all the governmental "craziness" by returning my attention to the Oneness of all things.

**Keep acting
and not reacting
to every little thing
that everyone would like
you to react to.**

Taking responsibility for our own actions, and holding our attention on the At-One-Ment, instead of all the "craziness" going on out there, are the antidotes to everything that separates us. For when we're awakened to the Atonement, we know, beyond all doubt, that nobody else is doing it to us. We're doing it all to ourself.

No More Buttons

One thing is certain. We can't move forward as long as we're judging everyone and everything around us. If we're going to reach our highest fulfillment, we'll eventually have to pull in the reins on our judging. Fortunately, the Universe will easily send us all the opportunities we need so we can practice withholding our judgments. There's no shortage of people and challenging situations that will push our buttons. It's when we learn to embrace these emotionally charged, button-pushing situations that we're released from them.

You're becoming more than a human being.
You're becoming a Universal Being.

BJ used to say that God is all inclusive. The name of the game of life, he said, is to embrace the things that have been blocking us from experiencing our Atonement. He said if there is something or someone we're avoiding, then that's the very person or situation we need to deal with in order to remove the blocks between us and our Ascension. (Note: Ascension, Atonement, God, Unity, Oneness, and The One are our favorite terms for the same Heavenly Experience. We use them interchangeably throughout this handbook.)

When I first met BJ he told me that I had "buttons" keeping me from experiencing the fullness of who I truly am. He said that there's something wonderful that awaits me after I've dealt with all my buttons. At the time this was all new to me. I didn't have the slightest idea what he was talking about. "Buttons!" I said. "Exactly what do you mean by my buttons, BJ?"

"Your buttons are the things you don't want to look at," he replied. "They're the experiences, brought on by past wounds, that you've been led to believe are wrong. When these past experiences happened, you didn't want them to happen, so you built up physical or emotional charge that lodged in places in your body which are now causing you pain or blockage. Once you remove these blockages, you're body will begin to heal itself and

function normally again."

"I'm still not sure what you're talking about, BJ. Can you give me an example?"

"Sure," he said, matter-of-factly. "Remember when you made an ass out of yourself last Thanksgiving carving the turkey? You wanted to impress that tough guy in the corner, so you served him up half the turkey and left hardly anything for the rest of us. Remember how it felt when we were all glaring at you?"

I knew exactly what he was talking about. I felt horrible after that incident. It was one of the most embarrassing moments of my life. I don't know what got into me at that neighborhood Thanksgiving party.

"Do you see the feelings it brings up when I remind you of that fiasco? It doesn't feel good, does it? That's because you're still carrying the emotional charge from that ridiculous incident with you. Like so much excess baggage, it's unresolved and blocking you from feeling good all the time. You even get jumpy and defensive when I mention it. That's what happens when one of your buttons is pushed."

Now I was starting to get the picture. "How do I do it, BJ," I asked him. "How do I get rid of the emotional charge?"

"You need somebody to push your buttons," he said.

I remember those words as if it was yesterday because they had such a powerful influence on me over the next 18 years. We were sitting at his kitchen table, overlooking the entire west coast of the island, as he went on with his explanation.

"We all have buttons in us," he said. *"Most people go through their entire lives carrying their buttons, not realizing that they're there. In most cases, they've build up a fortress of barriers they hide behind so they won't have to confront their buttons. Occasionally, however, you meet someone who truly wants to know what life is like on the other side of their buttons, and they'll seek out someone else to deliberately push their buttons. The one thing you want to make sure of is to pick someone who pushes your buttons lovingly."*

"Why is that?" I asked. I had no idea where he was going with this line of reasoning.

"Because," he said with a wry smile, *"getting your buttons pushed is not always a fun proposition. Until you get the handle on your knee-jerk reactions, it can make you mad as hell when your buttons are getting pushed. The key is to remember that you made a conscious decision in the first place, when you agreed to have your buttons pushed. The person who*

is deliberately pushing your buttons must have your permission before you ever get started."

And that's how it all began for me. I gave BJ permission to push my buttons, and I can assure you that he was right about there being times when I wanted to scream and run away, or even worse. Sometimes he'd push a button and I'd crawl back to my little coffee shack in the woods and tell myself I never wanted to see him again. But later, when I'd come back out of my hobbit hole and confront him, his response was always the same.

"You said you wanted to do this, Tony," he'd say. "You wanted to know what was on the other side of your buttons. You gave me your permission."

Looking back on it all, after 18 years of having my buttons consciously pushed on a daily basis, they're mostly gone. I still have a few, but, nowadays, I don't need BJ to show me my buttons. Life itself brings the perfect opportunities for me to deal with them. The system I use has shifted a bit over the years, as well, but the results are much the same. I used to crawl into my hermitage and ask myself, "what's not alright with this button being pushed?" That would bring up a past experience that wasn't previously alright with me so I could rewrite it with a happy ending.

These days, however, when one of my buttons brings

up an unresolved past wound, I do something that works even quicker. I welcome it and express my gratitude for it. It's just easier that way. Gratitude automatically balances everything out, without me having to wallow through the depths of my old blockages to do it. I'm even grateful for BJ pushing my buttons all those years, although I was screaming mad at the time. Sometimes we have to go through the madness in order to get to the miracle.

**Be open to all opportunities,
because sometimes
they come in different packages
than you are expecting.**

Gratitude for Everything

We tend to think of gratitude only when we have something good happen to us. We're thankful for our gifts, but what about expressing our gratitude for our adverse experiences and circumstances? What about expressing our gratitude for our pain and suffering? What about being grateful for our losses? After all, our adversity makes us stronger when we're able to look at it with gratitude in our heart and mind.

What about being grateful for everything that happens in our lives? When we're in a state of constant gratitude, no matter whether we think we've been helped or harmed, we open the door for healing to occur. For when we reflect on our past painful experiences with an attitude of sincere gratitude, we discover that the blockages lodged in our bodies from past wounds go away. That which was once lodged is now loosened; that which was once blocked is now healed.

We know that this idea is foreign to most folks. Most of us think we couldn't possibly be grateful for something painful that happened to us in the past. But we can. We can see the gift in it, and, in doing so, we find that it's much easier to heal a wound after a period of time than it is to heal it on the spot. When it first happens, we tend to get caught up in the shock of the situation. But as time passes, the shock goes away, and the door is opened for gratitude to work its miracles.

Here's how our friend, Dawn Katar, put it in a recent Point of Peace message she received from Archangel Raphael.

"The next time you think of the pain you have experienced in your past, infuse that memory with Peace. Whatever the pain, physical or emotional, recognize that while it felt real to you when you first experienced it, it is now a more pliable energy and when you give the pain gratitude you are able to heal all points of the pain - past, present and future."

**Everyone is a healer
and healing begins in thought.**

Not Guilty

One of the chief features of humankind is that we think we're doing things wrong. Or, we think that things are wrong in our world. In either case, our lives are riddled with wrongness, but nothing could be further from the truth. For, wrongness comes from the ego. It's something we're taught. It isn't intrinsically part of whatever we're perceiving. We bought into this strange idea when we were kids and started putting our judgment on everything around us. Over time, we allowed it deep into our lives, and now we find that our happiness depends on us extricating ourselves from it. Why? Because it's the Great Separator, keeping us apart from one another and keeping us from experiencing who we really are. It keeps us from our Ascension.

Wrongness, or guilt, runs much deeper in us than we know, and all of our buttons are spun from it. Unbeknownst to us, it pervades every decision we make and sabotages us at every turn. Buried deep in our psyche, it causes us pain and suffering for the whole of our lives, holding us at a low vibratory level until we uncover it and get rid of it. At its core, it makes us feel dense and sluggish compared to how we feel when it goes away. For when it's gone, we feel lighter, happier. We feel expanded and free.

BJ and I sat on the roof of the small coffee shack we were building in the rainforest, taking a break while I berated myself for nailing the last sheet of corrugated roofing on crooked. As I was going through my emotional gyrations, he was cool and centered - even though we'd have to pull the angled sheet of roofing off and replace it. It was a precarious job we wouldn't need to be doing, if it wasn't for my screw-up.

"You think you're doing things wrong, Tony. In fact, you think all sorts of things can go wrong. But when

you reach a higher level of awareness you'll see that nothing is wrong, never has been wrong, and never will be wrong. It's all a fabrication of your mind that you've bought into by believing what you were told by your parents and teachers and the TV."

"That may be true, BJ, but I just don't see it." I was still fuming over my mistake.

"Believe me, it's true," he said, "and if you're going to reach a higher level of awareness, you're going to have to come to grips with it."

"But how can I come to grips with something I don't know anything about," I asked.

"Start to pay greater attention when you think something's gone wrong in your life," he replied. "You won't have to wait long, I assure you, because it happens all the time, just like it did with that piece of tin roof you messed up. Then, when you're in the thick of your uncomfortable experience, like you are now, ask yourself, 'Where did this anger or discomfort come from? What's not alright with this happening?' Then be quiet and be open to receive your answer. Your memory will jog back to an experience you had when you were younger that's been covered over and almost forgotten about."

I put my hammer aside and sat still, and, almost immediately, a subtle thought flashed across my mind taking me back to a scene in my dad's workshop where he'd made a bad cut on a length of 2x4. He was cussing like crazy - and little 8 year old me was sympathizing with him because I believed he'd done something wrong.

"Now what do I do, BJ?"

"Shine your light on that memory long enough for it to melt away. Remember your innate innocence and let go of any judgment you're holding around it. It just happened and that's all. There's no need for you to put your spin on it. Soon it will disappear into nothingness, or it will domino your mind to another similar experience you had where you go through the same thing again, releasing your judgment and recalling your innate innocence. When all of the dominos have fallen – and this can happen very quickly – you'll find out what's on the other side of your wrongness and guilt."

"And what's that, BJ?" By this time I was starting to feel better about the roofing. Recalling the incident in my dad's workshop must have had something to do with my emotional turnaround.

"You, Tony, in all your radiant Oneness," he said. "What you'll find, buried underneath all the guilt and wrongdoing, is you."

The opposite of guilt is innocence. If we're going to get rid of our deep seeded guilt, we need to claim our innocence on an on-going basis. We must realize, at the core of our Being, that we're not doing anything wrong and have never done anything wrong. We were born pure and loving, without a shred of wrongdoing in our mind, and that's the place we need to get back to.

Ascension Reclamation #1

==
I Reclaim my Innocence
I've never done anything wrong and neither has anyone else. I forgive myself for thinking otherwise, and I let go of my guilt and self condemnation forever. I reclaim my innocence now.
==

Perfection

Most people have to stretch their thinking a bit in order to talk about the perfection in all things. However, once this "rogue" idea takes hold in us, we find that it's comforting because it explains why some of us experience suffering, while others live high on the hog. The culprit, when we think about things being less than perfect, lies in comparing ourselves to one another. Indeed, we do ourselves a tremendous disservice when we play the comparison game because, when we compare ourself to someone else, we are fundamentally creating an "us and them" scenario that takes us a step further away from experiencing the Atonement so many of us long for. Comparing ourself to others inherently separates us from each other, and from The One.

Before we go any further, let's explain what we mean by all things being perfect. It means that everything is going along fine, just as it is. No judgment is required on our part. The people who need to learn what it's like to be rich are experiencing that, and the people who need to suffer in order to accomplish what they came to Earth to accomplish are doing that. We're all in the perfect environment for doing what we came here to do. So, you might ask, how can a person who is in pain be in a state of perfection?

Everybody is getting what they need.
It may not look like it, but it's true.

This is the point where we're called upon to stretch our thinking. We have to look at the bigger picture. We have to look at our existence in eternity, as opposed to fixating on this one lifetime. So let's draw a line right now. If you believe that this life you're living is the only life there is, and that you came out of nowhere and return to nowhere after you die, then you can stop reading right now. If, however, you believe (or know) that your journey began long before this lifetime and that your Essence, the invisible core of you who resides deep inside your body, goes on long after you leave the body, then keep reading because that which follows is meant to help you.

Here, it serves us to make a distinction between our soul and our Spirit, or Essence. Our soul is the part of us that connects our body with our Essence. It monitors and regulates our many bodily experiences, making sure we stay on the path we set for ourselves in between lifetimes. Our Essence, on the other hand, is who we are at our core. Our Essence is unchangeable and lives forever. We cannot fail to return to our Essence because we really never leave It. It just gets covered over with all the dense debris we attach

65

to ourselves throughout our many lifetimes. Fortunately for us, all of our lessons lead to the same place. They lead to our soul's growth and eventually back to our Essence, not necessarily to our personal wealth or immediate satisfaction.

In terms of our physical lives, our soul knows what's best for us. Before we come here to Earth, we take stock of what we need to learn, and we put ourselves in what we think will be the perfect situation for getting rid of our lower tendencies and raising our inner frequency as high as we can. Some people come here to learn one lesson and move on, while others bite off more than they can chew and try to cram a whole slew of lessons into one lifetime. The point with this is that comparing ourself to others makes no sense in light of our soul's growth. We're all exactly where we're supposed to be. Our ego may not think so, but our soul watches over us in every instant and does it's level best to keep us on the track we set for ourself before we came here. When we listen to our ego and wander off track, our soul realizes that we haven't learned our lessons yet, and it adapts, creating new scenarios designed to bring us back in line with our original plans.

Clearly, the people who are here on Earth at this time are in vastly different stages of learning their lessons. Some folks are loving and are very near graduation, while others have brought great anger in with them, or have perpetrated horrific acts on their fellowmen and women. (Please understand that we are not judging anyone as good or bad or right or wrong, regardless of what they've done. We are, however, saying that they may have a longer row to hoe before they graduate out of the cycle of 3D embodiment.) In order to graduate they have to balance out their hateful acts - and, for some, the only way to do this is to experience the exact same pain and suffering that they perpetrated on others. They have to know what it's like to be hurt so they will stop hurting others. It's that simple.

Thus, from our soul's perspective, we're all getting exactly what we need in every moment. Our ego, the instigator of all our painful experiences, may be crying out in protest, but our soul knows that it's all happening perfectly. Not one step we take is out of place. It's all leading us back to our Ascension. It's all leading us Home.

You have to trust that there is a Higher Power at work in your life and in your world.

Ascension Reclamation #2

==

I Reclaim my Perfection

I am perfect and so is everyone else. I see all of us getting exactly what we most need for our soul's growth in every moment. Everything is right on schedule. No judgments or comparisons are required on my part. I reclaim my perfection and the perfection of all things now.

==

Patience and the Yet Factor

The world is moving fast and it seems like it's moving faster by the day. People are walking faster, talking faster, driving faster, pushing on one another, often without regard for anyone else around them. It's like we live in a buzz, especially in the more urban areas, and it's making people more impatient. Those who are intending for peace sometimes feel like we're having our frequencies jammed by all the speediness going on around us.

Fortunately, there's an opportunity for us in all of this fast-paced activity. It provides us with the perfect environment in which to cultivate patience. If we can learn to wait patiently while the world is chaotic all around us, we will have brought ourself closer to the inner peace we seek. In other words, if we can do it here, we can do it anywhere.

BJ was a Taurus, like a bull, willing to wait forever for whatever he wanted. Back in those days on our avocado farm / mystery school, I was fresh out of the Honolulu mainstream, full of hiss and vinegar. I wanted everything yesterday and had little patience for anything that got in the way of me getting what I wanted as quickly as possible. I needed to slow down and didn't have the slightest idea how to do it.

One rainy Hawaiian afternoon, BJ and I were driving back to the farm in my 64 Dodge Power Wagon. It was a strong older truck, perfect for our small farming needs, but it was getting tired. When we were coming up the steepest part of the road from Kailua to Kainaliu, it started sputtering and we had to pull over to let it cool down.

"It needs an overhaul," BJ said, as we sat by the side of the road watching the cars go by. "It's a good truck, but it won't last another year unless we take the engine apart, lap the valves, do the rings and clean it up from top to bottom."

Well, I was a college boy with a major in money and banking, and I didn't have the slightest idea what he was taking about. Lap the valves, what the heck was that? "BJ," I said, "I've always gone to a mechanic whenever I had car trouble. No one ever taught me the first thing about engines. I've never taken one apart and wouldn't know where to begin. I am willing to learn, though." Since we lived way back in the hills, I knew there would be times in the future when I needed these skills. He'd told me previously that a Master gets good at a lot of skills; that he worked at one thing just long enough to get really good at it, and then he went on the next thing. In this way, a Master amasses many talents and abilities and is more prepared to deal with any new projects or challenges that come his or her way.

"I'm a mechanic and I'll help you," he said. "I'll teach you how to do an overhaul. We can start tomorrow, if you'd like. It shouldn't take us more than a week."

Well, this was great news for me. The only problem was that I had a nice little landscaping business that was paying the monthly bills, and I needed the truck to do my work. So, that night, I called the people on my landscaping route and asked them if it was okay if I skipped a week. I told them that I had to overhaul my truck, that I really appreciated their business, and

that I'd make it up to them if they'd keep me on as their
weekly landscaper. To my great relief, they all agreed.

The next day, bright and early, BJ and I cleared out
a space on the side of the overgrown country road that
ran through our property and went to work. By mid
morning, we had the top of the engine off and various
cans filled with parts soaking in gasoline to get the black
crusty oil deposits off of them. I watched BJ carefully as
I sat on an upside-down white 5 gallon plastic bucket,
lapping valves. By the end of the day, we had the
engine completely apart and were surrounded by piles
of parts not-so-neatly arranged by the order in which
they came out of the engine compartment. We agreed
to meet early the next morning and start putting it all
back together.

The following morning, I got down to the truck at
7am and resumed my work on the valves. Apparently
BJ decided to sleep in because he hadn't shown up yet.
By ten o'clock he still hadn't shown, so I walked up the
hill to see what was keeping him. I found a note on his
kitchen table saying "Gone Fishing with da boys. See
you tomorrow." Well, I could understand this. We were
friends with 3 brothers who were fisherman, and, when
the fish were running, they sometimes called to see if

we wanted to join them on the boat.

I walked back down the hill and looked around me at the parts spread around the ground. What a mess! There was no way I could possibly begin to put it all back together on my own. I didn't even know where to start! I finished with the valves, and the rest would have to wait until tomorrow, when BJ got back.

The next morning, no BJ. The same note sat on the table. It hadn't moved. I didn't know what to do, so I went to the orchard and pruned some fruit trees, all the while silently cussing BJ and hoping that we could get the truck done by the weekend so I could get back to my landscaping customers on Monday.

Long story short, the entire week went by and BJ was nowhere to be seen. He showed up the following week, but was uncharacteristically ill and spent the next several days in bed reading and watching his tiny 12 volt black and white TV. He apologized for the delay and said we'd get back to the truck as soon as he was completely well. Of course, I was angry, but it didn't do me any good. I had to call my customers again and even lost a couple of them. All I could do was wait.

After an ongoing series of his excuses, an entire month went by before we got back to work on the truck. In the meantime, all of my customers left me for other landscaping *services, and I'd gone through every emotion imaginable. During the fourth week, however, something started to shift in me: the truck issue wasn't bothering me like before. I was learning that it was all right if I had to wait. I found other things to do while I was waiting, and I began to notice that the speediness I'd brought to the country with me was going away. I was learning to be patient.*

In the long run, I found another source of income that was even more enjoyable and lucrative than landscaping in the subdivisions. It didn't matter anymore that I lost those customers; in fact, it was a gift. New doors opened for me while I was waiting, and I learned that just because something hadn't happened YET, didn't mean it wasn't going to happen. Oh, and I learned something else of great value, too. I learned that what BJ told me about the Masters was true. The Masters are good at all sorts of things, not just mechanics or construction. They're also skilled at the fine art of communication. They can even make use of an old truck to teach their apprentice how to be patient.

FYI: It wasn't until a couple of years later that I flashed on what it must have taken for BJ to put on an act like that in order to teach me patience. Yes, it was an act, a role he played out so I would learn something of much greater benefit to me than knowing how to fix a truck. I learned that going past the predetermined deadlines I'd set for how long I thought something was going to take didn't need to interfere with my inner equilibrium. I can be at peace, no matter how long I have to wait.

Money and fame are not really the judging factors of success. That's the ego at work. Most people are looking outside themselves to measure their success, but success and joy are an inside job.

Playing a Role

What stops many people from manifesting their dreams is the gap between where they think they are now and where they want to go. They think they're stuck in the situation they're in, and that it's highly unlikely they'll ever get out of it. We see this all the time in our Intenders Circles, and, when it comes up, we always do our best to raise the bar by helping them phrase their intentions with the most positive outcome we can think of. Sometimes they're able go along with our recommendations, and sometimes they're not ready to make such a big leap.

This situation not only happens in our Intenders Circles; it also happens out in the world. We think things will never change for us. The light at the end of the tunnel seems so far away that we tend to resign ourselves to enduring the status quo. In these instances, those of us who have been integrating these empowering principles into our daily lives often turn to an old, tried-and-true method in order to shake off the inertia we're creating for ourselves. We act as if. We fake it till we make it.

Of course, these are old clichés, so often undermined by those around us - *but they work*. In fact, they're an integral part of the manifestation process. When we "act as if", we're actually creating that which we desire for ourself because we're envisioning it. Here's how it works. Whatever we're picturing in our mind is working its way toward the surface of our daily experience - even if it doesn't necessarily agree with what's going on in our outer world. For example, just because we only have two dollars in our pocket doesn't mean we can't be thinking that we have two thousand. We can think whatever we want, regardless of the circumstances around us.

In this respect, at a certain point in our evolution, we're called upon to learn to play a role, just like an actor or actress in Hollywood. We have to act like we already have that which the world would tell us is lacking. Fortunately, we need not convince others, but we must convince ourselves that we already have what we want; for indeed, *in our mind,* we do.

There is no lack in our mind unless we allow it to be there. We can think anything we want whenever we want - and, from there, it's only a matter of time before our thoughts manifest outwardly into our everyday life.

The way to go to the next level is to live it now.

Ascension Reclamation #3

===
I Reclaim my Power
The mainstream reality doesn't affect me unless I allow it to do so. I am thinking whatever I want and thus creating whatever I want. By envisioning only positive outcomes, I reclaim my power now.
===

Accepting

One of the most challenging things we learned in the Intenders is that there are some intentions that don't manifest for us. Perhaps we'd been intending for something specific to come to us and, after a long period of time, it just hadn't happened. In this instance, we discovered that it wasn't for our Highest Good to have manifested yet - and we learned to accept it and go on with our lives. The trick, we found, is to be happy in the meantime, to keep our emotional balance even though we have to go without some of the things we think we need.

You see, many of us had control issues. We wanted to be able to manifest whatever we desired - and, according to the Law of Attraction, we can do this. Indeed, our thoughts do create our future, but the timing is another matter. Sometimes the Universe knows that it's not in our best interests on a soul level for us to manifest certain intentions at a particular time. If this were to happen, we would be putting our soul's purpose in jeopardy. We'd be sabotaging our own future.

***The path is to go within, to listen,
to allow the next thing to show itself to you.***

Indeed, we come into this lifetime with a plan, our soul's plan, and, at some point, if we're following our heart, it's revealed to us. Then, as long as we stay with it, we will accomplish what we set out to do here on planet Earth, which, for many, is to go Home in this lifetime. What we didn't bargain for was all the temptations along the way.

I was brought up in a family where money was my parents primary focus in life. It's just about all they talked about. They wanted more of it; and when they got it, they still wanted more. Now, to a point, this is understandable because most of us have had previous lifetimes when we went hungry or were cold in the winter, and we've carried over memories from those times of poverty and scarcity into this life. That, coupled with the American money dream, which constantly programs us to want more than we need, caused many of us, myself included, to lose track of our soul's plan.

I grew up with the same values as my parents. In my early years and throughout college I prepared myself to make a lot of money. I even earned a degree in economics to further that endeavor. As it turned out, my parents fell into the same trap that haunts most Americans and had to use all of their savings to pay for their old age expenses, leaving none left over for me or my brother to jumpstart our adult lives. If I was going to live the dream of my childhood and accumulate a lot of money, I was going to have to do it on my own.

Long story short, it never happened. Throughout my entire adult life I've never had more than I needed at any given time. I've worked hard, played hard and fully enjoyed my life, but the money never came in amounts more than just enough to get by - and I had to learn to accept this, even though there were times when it frustrated me to the limit. It wasn't until I moved out to the country and started farming that I realized my soul had different plans for me, money-wise. I had to learn how to be happy regardless of how much money I had. It all started making sense when BJ told me that money need not be my measure of security; that my security was to be found in becoming a Mighty Manifester. As long as I learned to get proficient at manifesting and trust the Universe, I would gain a skill that is much more valuable to me than how to accumulate money.

From that moment on, I let go of the American money dream. I accepted whatever came to me, knowing it was exactly what I needed at the time. Oh sure, every-so-often I fell back into my old childhood habits of wanting more money. But, over time, these instances happened less and less. Looking back over my life now, I see that I always had everything I needed. I wrote 11 books, created and ran an intentional community that spans the entire globe, raised 3 boys, traveled the world - all without having ever taken on a permanent job. If I hadn't been able to accept my soul's plan, it's very likely that I would have lived a different life entirely. I'd probably be working for a weekly paycheck in a humdrum office somewhere. Instead, I learned to be resourceful and make do with what I had.

And you know what? So far, so good. There's always been enough.

The timing of your manifestations
is what's frustrating for many.
Our Higher Self doesn't operate off of ego.
It operates on Universal Timing,
and this is where acceptance comes in.
There is an order to the Universe
and we have to accept that order.

Letting Go

The last, and perhaps the most formidable, step in the manifestation process is letting go. We've seen this more times than we can count in our Intention Circles. People want what they want and are not willing to let go of their intention so an opening will be created for it to manifest. They hold on too tight, not realizing that by holding on, they are actively keeping their dreams and desires at bay.

***You don't really have to give it all up.
You just have to be willing to***.

It took us a long time to understand this principle because it's so intangible. We simply couldn't tell why some of our intentions weren't manifesting for us. We'd made clear intentions, suspended our disbelief, overcome our doubts, envisioned the final outcome, took action when the situation presented itself, waited, and waited some more - and still nothing happened. It wasn't until I had a private session with Lee Ching that things started making sense.

"I can't imagine why some of the things we've been intending for haven't manifested, Lee Ching. It could be that they're not for our Highest Good, but some of these intentions seem so harmless that it's hard to understand why it wouldn't be for our Highest Good if they manifested."

Tina and I were sitting in the small park adjacent to the natural volcanic warm ponds where she taught aqua aerobics to a lively group of ladies twice a week. The ladies had gone home, and I'd asked her if she would bring through Lee Ching for me because I had a few questions that were gnawing at me. (This was in the early days of the Intenders, before Lee Ching started coming through me.) We were all alone in one of the most beautiful settings on the island, with the waves lapping gently over the breakwater on the far side of the ponds. She said her prayer and, right away, the feeling that always accompanies Lee Ching settled over us.

"Tony, we both know that your greatest desire and intention in this life is to know God," he began. "Up to this point, you've had glimpses, and yet you haven't been able to make the connection with your Heavenly Father on a full time basis, and there is a reason for this." I wondered where he was going with this idea, *but I didn't interrupt because I felt so good in that moment and didn't want to lose the feeling.*

"There is an old adage," he continued, "about approaching God that will help you, and it goes like this: You can pray and meditate and try as hard as you can to find God, but it's not until you finally let go of your desire to know God, after doing all that you can do, that He comes to you."

Hmmm, I'd never looked at it like this before. I'd been doing everything I could think of - eating right, living in nature, praying, meditating everyday, studying, going to sacred places and more - but, except for a brief peak experience I'd had in the rainforest in Kona several years earlier, nothing had happened.

"You will know God, Tony, I promise you that." he said, smiling like he knew something I didn't - which, of course, he did. "I tell you this story only because it represents an example that will also shed light on why some of your other intentions haven't manifested yet. You can push as hard as you can, but there comes a time when you have to let go before you can enjoy the manifestation of your intentions. In order to have it all, you have to give it all up."

He went on to talk about trust and how letting go involved learning to trust at a much deeper level than

*ever before. He said that trust was one of the greatest
issues facing mankind today and that our Intenders
groups were forging new inroads into the culture by
learning that whatever we're intending will come to us
- if we let go and trust.*

That conversation took place over twenty years
ago and, after manifesting just about everything
I've intended since then, I still catch myself on a
regular basis having to deal with this issue. Some of
us are more stubborn about holding on than others,
and I'm as stubborn as any. Fortunately, whenever
I catch myself clinging too tightly to an intention,
I remember the conversation that day by the warm
ponds with Lee Ching, and I remind myself to let
go and let God.

*There's always a point
right before things manifest for you,
right before you get what you want,
when you'll notice that there's a letting go,
and you're telling yourself,
"It's OK if I do get what I want
and it's OK if I don't get what I want."*

What God Created and What We Created

Most folks are pretty confused about God and what He created. They hear that God is all loving and so they can't understand why He'd create a world where there's so much suffering and chaos. The truth is: He didn't create the mess we're in. We did. God didn't have anything to do with it, except that He allowed us to do it.

Ask yourself, would a God who loves us and cares for us make war? Would a God who wouldn't condemn a soul create a system that has us all feeling guilty? Would a loving God spray us with toxins, bomb innocent civilians, tax us beyond our ability to pay, charge us for being sick, foreclose on our houses, take away our hard-earned pensions, lie at every opportunity, torture, maim and kill anyone who doesn't go along with the party line? The answer is a resounding NO. A loving God would never do these things. But we would. We created the world where these horrible things are going on. The question is: how could this happen?

It started when we were children. You see, when we're young, we tend to believe our elders. We can't imagine that they'd do anything that would bring us harm. So we bought into their ways and started to act like them. If we stepped out of line, we were punished or ridiculed in front of our friends. At the time, we were too young to understand that there are people running this Earth, and that they'd set everything up so they could be in charge and control everyone else. When we finally figured out what was going on, we were so entrenched in it all that we couldn't get out of it without great hardship or risk to ourselves.

> *Once people realize that they're the ones who created the mess in their life, they'll begin to straighten it out.*

Meanwhile, behind the scenes, God, in His love, is letting us run our own show. He doesn't interfere because that would be unloving and controlling. He knows we want to live in peace, but that we have lessons to learn from having been acculturated to all the suffering and strange behavior here. He gives us the freedom to learn our lessons, regardless of how harsh they may seem. In short, it's not Him doing it to us. It's us doing it to ourselves.

Perhaps because they were said with such strong emotion behind them, the very first words that registered with me in this life were "God damn it." My father yelled them in anger as I sat in the back seat of our old 52 Desoto. We are parked at the Dairy Queen, and I think he spilled some of his chocolate-dipped cone in his lap, but I'm not really sure. All I know is he was very mad and condemning God for it.

As I was growing up, I found that these words were used regularly by the people around me. It was especially common to hear them in the movies, and it seemed like the people who used them needed some extra attention. Even later, as I began to use them myself, I realized that I said them because I wanted to emphasize what I was saying. It made me look stronger, like I was unafraid of God, even though, at that time in my life, I didn't have any thoughts about God yet. I didn't even know what I was saying. I was just repeating what my father was saying to get more attention.

I didn't go to church when I was a child. My parents were not religious and never talked about spiritual things. They were only interested in money, and they left me alone to find out about God on my own. It wasn't until I read <u>A Course in Miracles</u> that I realized that God doesn't condemn. It's us, with our constant *swearing and cussing, doing all the condemning. If I wanted to be more like God, I would have to stop condemning things every time I got angry. First and foremost, I would have to stop damning God because He wasn't the One who was doing anything to anger me. It was me who was making myself mad. The challenge was not with God, or with anyone else. The challenge was in my own mind. I could choose to project my anger outward, like all victims tend to do, or I could own my anger and choose to see things differently.*

Nowadays I don't cuss like before - not because I'm not angry on occasion (everyone gets angry now and then) - but because I'm being more careful about what I'm creating with my everyday words. Why would I ever want to condemn God or condemn others in His name? I wouldn't, because it'll never give me the results I'm looking for. I'll never know what love is as long as I'm condemning anything or anyone else, including God.

God gives us freedom to create as we choose.
We can create beauty or we can create chaos.
The choice is up to us.

Two Voices

When we listen closely we find that there are two voices in our head. One is from our ego and the other is from Our Higher Self / The Holy Spirit / Jesus Christ / The Voice for God. The one we hear the most is our ego, and although it would have us think that it's our best buddy, it definitely is not. In fact, the ego is our worst enemy, doing its utmost at all times to get us to do things that don't serve us. Our Higher Self, on the other hand, is totally loving and truly cares for our well being; it's just that it is more subtle and not as easy to hear, what with all the noise blaring from the ego.

In other words, until we make a strong connection with our Higher Self, our ego is the voice we're hearing most of the time. We can tell it from our Higher Self because it's louder, angrier, vengeful, deceptive, judgmental, reactive, fixated on glamour, hierarchal, morose, contradictory and, most of all, separative. It is the voice for the body, having us think that it is the body, when, in fact, it is nothing more than an impermanent voice in our head. We can always tell when it's in play by how we feel, for the feeling that accompanies it is not loving or caring, but self-righteous and sabotaging. In many ways, it's like the keeper at the gate of our mind, doing everything it can to keep us from going through the gate to where our glory resides.

Once we get past the gate, however, the voice of The Holy Spirit / Higher Self / Jesus Christ awakens in us, and we have a friend and helper available to us. Of course, It's always been there; we just couldn't hear It before because of all the ego's clamoring. Now we have access to all the answers in the Universe. We rediscover our innate creativity and so much more. All things are possible with the help of The Holy Spirit, if we will but call It forth - and that's the challenge for most people. We're so caught up in the ego and all its distractions that we neglect to make contact with the highest and best part of us.

Fortunately, people today are becoming disenchanted with the ego's questionable motives, and they're looking for something that truly offers happiness and upliftment. The ego has not and can not provide these things. Only our Higher Self can bring peace and joy into our lives. The trick is getting past the ego, and we do this by quieting our mind long enough for the ego to shut down and our Higher Self to make Itself known. For once the mind is stilled, the Voice of our Higher Self comes clear. How will we know it? It's the one that is sweet, sincere, gentle but strong, caring, all-knowing, helpful, guiding us to our highest fulfillment, guiding us back Home.

The Moody Blues said it so beautifully: *"It's not the way that you say it when you do those things to me. It's more the way you really mean it when you tell me what will be."* That's how you can tell whether the voice you're hearing is from the ego or The Holy Spirit: The Holy Spirit is the One who really means it when It tells you what will be.

The real revolution is in consciousness.
When you change your consciousness
you help balance out
what's very awry in your world
- the injustice, the impropriety, the lying.
People are realizing that these things
are not really okay
and they don't want
to be part of them anymore.

Quiet Time

Really busy people aren't any happier. Happiness is not to be found by running around and doing things all the time. We need to stop occasionally, and, just like we need to digest our food, we need to digest our experiences. Especially when we've undergone highly emotional situations, it's wise for us to take time to rid ourself of our emotional charge, lest we explode and dump it on those around us. You see this happen everyday. People are tweaked, carrying too much emotional baggage, and they're looking to rid themselves of it anywhere and anyway they can. This leads to all sorts of ugly dramas and miscreations.

So, what can we do with our charge? How do we get rid of it without dumping it on our friends and neighbors? The answer is this: we use it for our positive creativity or we take quiet time. Either one will help us balance out our emotional charge, but there's no substitute for taking time to ourself in silence. We set aside time everyday to do nothing: no reading, no writing, no counting, no thinking, no doing. We take a break from the world outside us, and we look inside for awhile. If a thought arises, we treat it like a passing cloud and gently let it go by on its own. Simply doing this releases much of the charge we've built up during the day. There are many methods of meditation you can check into, and some are designed to fast-track you, but sitting in a quiet place, closing your eyes (without falling asleep), and doing absolutely nothing for awhile will help you immensely.

You'll be surprised how much better you feel after taking some quiet time each day. You'll find a peace inside yourself that will begin to show itself outside of you, as well. Your relationships will go smoother, and your work environment will improve because people need to work with people who are coming from a calm, reserved, meditative state of mind. You will be able help others in ways that were previously unavailable to you when you were so busy.

And who knows, perhaps somewhere along the line, you'll discover something inside yourself that you didn't notice there before. A whole new world opens up and calls you to explore deeper, further . . .

There is a part of you that is unfathomable.

Part III
Breaking the Spells
The Body and the Dream

Most of us think we are our body. But, again, nothing could be further from the truth. Just because we believed our parents and teachers when they told us that we are our body doesn't mean it's true. And just because almost everyone else we've ever met supports and agrees with this idea doesn't mean it's real. It's not. It's just another illusion we harbor. It's just a dream.

The very first question BJ asked me when I started my apprenticeship in our isolated Hawaiian mystery school was, "Tony, are you your body?" Well, it caught me by surprise. I stood there speechless for a moment, thinking. Nobody had ever asked me anything like this before. He could see I was befuddled, so he shifted gears. "Then, are you your hands?" he asked.

This time I answered straight away. "No," I said. This was easier because I knew I was more than my hands, and, unlike his first question, it didn't confront the strong attachment I had to my lifelong identification

94

with the body.

Seeing my inner wheels spinning, he went on, "Are you your feet, then?" Again, I replied right away with an even more emphatic "No" - but now something started to shift inside me. If I wasn't my hands, and I wasn't my feet, then could it be that I am not the rest of my body, either? And if if this is true, what am I, really?

We called it "flashing" - like a flash of light, or a new insight, that hits us. He knew not to say another word while I was "flashing" and, in the silence that followed, my whole life changed. If I'm not my body, who or what am I? I must be something or someone inside my body because I know that I exist. Something or someone is animating, bringing to life, everything I'm experiencing. What could it be?

Let's look at this illusion a little closer to see how it works. When we get out of bed in the morning, we look out of our eyes at the world around us. The thing we generally notice first is our body because it's the closest thing to us. Then, as we look further out into the world, we see the objects in our room and the scene outside our windows. It's at this point where we make a distinction between the body and everything else we see. We create a separation between the body and the things beyond it, saying to ourself that we are "our" body and everything else is "the world".

That's one way of looking at it. There is also another way of looking at this illusion that most people never notice. We can just as easily look out of our eyes and see everything in our view impersonally. We need not make the distinction between the body and everything else. We need not separate our body out from the other things we see. And we need not identify with the body, thinking that it is who we are. It's just another object that's in our view, a view seen from the mind, not from our eyes. Indeed, the eyes are just another part of the body.

One cloudy afternoon BJ told me that there are two ways to perceive things. In one way, when we look out at the world, we see our body, and then we see everything else that extends outward from our body in the form of objects and other people. In this view, we assume that we are our body and everything else we see is separate from it. He said this is how most people look at the world.

The second way of perceiving has us looking out at the

world and seeing no separation whatsoever between the body and everything else. It's all just an ever-changing scene we're witnessing. From this viewpoint, there's no need for us to identify with the body because we're placing no more importance on it than anything else we're seeing. It's just another object in our view, not unlike the furniture or the mountains in the distance.

BJ went on to say that an interesting thing happens after we've looked at the world in this second way for awhile: the objects in our view begin to merge into One. We see it as all as being connected into one homogenous whole - and it's at this point where we begin to question our true identity. Since we're no longer identifying with the body, then who or what can we identify with?

See if you can answer this for yourself: If you're not your body, then who or what are you?

Here's a hint: *you're invisible.*

We think we are seeing with our eyes but, in reality, we're seeing with our mind. It's easier to understand this uncommon idea when we look at how dreams work. When we're in a dream at night, our eyes are closed, and yet we're seeing all sorts of things happening around us. Clearly, we do not

97

need our eyes to see these things because they're closed while we're dreaming. That means we must be seeing everything with our mind.

So what makes us think that it's any different when we awaken in the morning? Could it be that we're still seeing everything from our mind? Could it be that our physical body is just another prop in the movie we call "the world", and that there is no distinction, no separation, between the body and the rest of the world we see, unless we choose to believe it is so?

The challenge with actually experiencing this radical new point of view lies in the longstanding agreements we have with each other here on Earth. It's traditional for us to identify with our body because almost everyone else is doing it. We have to become a true renegade in order to look past the illusion. We must be able to forge a new path and see beyond the cultural dream. It takes a person who, when she sees the body, can tell herself, *"It's not me! I'm not this body! I'm so much more than this body! It's just another prop in the movie I'm projecting! I'm the One in the projection room! I'm the Essence who resides in the body who runs the whole show!"*

So let's have some fun. Go ahead. Right now.

Look out at the scene before you. You see arms and hands and the front of the body - and you see everything else that's beyond it. What makes you think that the body you're seeing is any different from everything else in your view? What is it that makes you want to separate it out from the rest of the scene you're witnessing? And why, then, would you want to call it "you" and identify with it?

You don't have to, you know.

The new awareness is about being One with everything and everyone.

The Separation

From our normal earthly point of view, it looks like we're surrounded by objects. We see the chair, or the table, or the hills in the distance, and so forth - and we think that these things are separate from each other. At least, that's what we've been taught. We also make another distinction as we look upon an object that's in our view: we think we're separate from it; that there's us and there is the object itself, with space between us and it. As we said, this is the way most people perceive things.

In addition, we've been educated to put a label on all the things we see around us. We give names to everything, and this practice solidifies the idea that things are divided from one another. These divisions multiply as objects are given names, names are made up of words, and words are made up of letters that we string together using a process we call spelling. It's at this point where some teachers would say *a spell was cast*; that the moment when we first began to create and use words was the exact same moment we began to separate ourselves from all that surrounds us. The question that arises out of this is: what was going on just prior to the time the spell was cast? What were we doing before we were separated?

The Bible says "In the beginning was the Word." There are many who would say that the "Word" was the beginning of the separation, and that, before the use of words, we were at One with All That Is. Think about it for a moment. What were you perceiving before you learned to use words? You existed, didn't you? You were breathing and wiggling around, but you didn't have a name that you knew of, or a story about yourself. You were simply cradled in the loving embrace of a new world that encompassed all and everything. You were at One with all of It.

From that vantage point, we can see that we've existed in at least two worlds: the world before words when we were One, and the world that came after that when we bought into the words and started playing the separation game. Most of us don't remember when we were One, but we do know a great deal about the separation game. Indeed, we've gotten very good at it. The Mayans called it the illusion, and they said it only exists because we believe in it; that it's our perception that makes it seem real. According to them, we could learn to experience the world around us in an entirely different way. We could learn to experience it all as One, as it was before the advent of words. This is the place our quantum scientists are coming to.

One thing that will help us is to realize that our Atonement didn't go away once we started playing the separation game. It's still here, there and everywhere, just waiting for us to tap back into It. It's as if the separation we think we're perceiving is embedded within The One, just like the coding in a webpage. We can't see the source code when we visit a webpage, but it's actively going on behind the scenes, directing our entire experience. In the same way, the objects and people we see around us are embedded within the Atonement, and it's up to us to shift our perception in order to experience It.

There are many paths, both religious and spiritual, that lead to this perceptual change, and you can find the one that works best for you. Regardless of which path you choose, however, each of them will eventually ask you to let go of the old way you've been perceiving things. We're asked to find a way to experience It like It once was before we began using words, before we became separated. The challenge with this is that we've become stuck in the separation game. We've gotten so attached to the objects and situations around us that it's as if we're under the spell of the illusion. How do we break the spell? By reclaiming our true identity.

Who you think you are
is very different
from who you really are.

Ascension Reclamation #4

===
I Reclaim my True Identity

I am much more than I've been led to believe.
No longer identified with my name, my story or
my body, I am the Essence embedded within this
body. I am Spirit, connected with my Creator
forever, unlimited and all knowing, immortal,
whole and holy. I am part and parcel of God, and
I reclaim my true identity now.

===

Your Story

The ego loves for us to tell our story. You have
your story and I have mine, but, in truth, they're
all pretty much the same. We talk about when and
where we were born, where we grew up, things
that happened in our childhood and teenage years,
where we went to school, how old we are, the jobs
we had, the relationships we had, the exciting
moments we had, and so forth. The more exciting
or surprising our experiences were, the more we
tend to tell others about them. They're the fodder
we use to make friends, the tools we use in order
to socialize.

But are they real? Are the stories we tell about ourselves real, or are they just another construct in our mind, another spell we're under?

BJ often said that it's easy to change the past. People do it all the time. We start to tell our story and, right away, we tend to exaggerate the way things really happened. We make it sound like it was bigger than it was, or how we were more heroic than we actually were. We do this, he said, because we want attention.

"Attention is love," he told me one evening while we were sitting at the picnic tables watching the sunset from the City of Refuge on the Kona side of the Big Island. "Love is putting your attention on another person the way they want it put on them. When you're giving your attention to someone else by letting them tell you their story, you're loving them. It's a great way to get to know people, and a great way for you to practice learning to love."

I thought about this new idea as the sun settled below the Pacific horizon. I could sure use more practice in the loving department. By letting others tell me their story, according to BJ, this is what I'd be doing.

"There's just one thing," he said with a smile. "Don't believe a word of it. It's just a story; it's not written in

stone. People will tell you all sorts of strange things in order to get your attention. They'll exaggerate like crazy! It doesn't matter, though. Your job is to learn to love them, not believe them. Besides...it's in the past. It's all in their mind. It's not in the Here and Now. You know what's going on in the Here and Now, don't you, Tony?"

Again, I had to stop and think. Where was he going with this? I looked down the beautiful beach; the waves rolled gently onto the shore.

"That's right," he said, without waiting for my answer. "What's going on in the Here and Now is we're sitting here chatting and watching this amazing sunset in one of the most sacred places on the planet. It's all happening right in front of us. Everything else is just a story in our mind."

If you're stuck in your thinking, go out and help someone, and you'll begin to feel again.

Getting Here from There

There's a great scene in the newest version of the movie *Total Recall* where our hero, Colin Farrell, after a long search, has just located the leader of the resistance, played by Bill Nighy. Farrell tells him about all the trials he's gone through to get there, and how they need to come up with a new strategy for taking their freedom from the oppressive governmental regime. Farrell said that they'd lose the war if they kept doing everything like they've always done in the past. Nighy's calm response was so poignant that it made my truth bell ring. His words were, *"My friend, the past is just a construct of the mind."*

Nighy was right. The past is just another trick the ego uses to keep us from experiencing the fullness of the Atonement. For when we're in a state of Oneness, we're in the Here and Now where the past and the future do not exist. In fact, the only place where these marvelous constructs of past and future do exist is in our mind. They're not outside of us, and can never be outside of us.

Inside of us, though, anything can happen. We can replay the same thought over in our mind as much as we like. We can project the same movie repeatedly. Our challenge with this is that we can get stuck in the past so deeply that we forget about the present. Yes, we do need to remember the past to the extent that it will keep us from repeating the experiences that didn't serve us. But too much rewinding to a past scene keeps us out of the Here and Now.

If we are to awaken to the majesty of the Atonement, we will need to stop replaying the same scene over and over, and refocus our attention on the present moment. For the present is where we find Reality with a capital R, while the past will only show us reality with a small r. Total Recall only happens when we're in the Here and Now.

People want to go back to the old ways
- where it's comfortable -
but we can't do this anymore.

The Story of the World

It's not much different when we tell the story of the world than when we're telling the story of the our life. Indeed, we know the story of the world quite well because we're telling it to our friends all the time. You know how it goes: we talk about the political scene, the wars, hard times and good times, what's on the nightly news, the latest sports scores, the latest movies, the latest entertainment gossip, and so on. Like everything else in the past, it's not in front of us in the Here and Now. It's only in our mind and can be rewritten anytime.

Ask yourself, where does this story about what's going on in our world come from? Who is responsible for bringing these subjects and events into our lives? Without naming names, you can be assured that those who are responsible for creating and keeping the story intact are the same people who want to be in control of the world. They want to control you and me, and will make up any story that suits their selfish purposes in order to do it. Our job is to discern. If the story we're being presented with feels good and serves us, then we can listen safely. But if, like most of the junk that's being dished out to us nowadays, it feels bad and doesn't serve us in the least, we actually harm ourselves by believing these stories and sharing them with our friends. This is why so many people are turning off their TVs these days. What they're blasting at us isn't in our best interests. It's in someone else's selfish interests.

The story of the world isn't true and isn't real. It's made up by people who want to manipulate the rest of us. It's all a propaganda scheme designed to take our power away and make us victims - and when we buy into the world's story, that's exactly what happens. We begin playing the blame game and instantly separate ourselves into camps. It's the same old stuff, so let's take a look at it from a new point of view.

What if we're projecting it all? What if the story of the world is of our own making, and we're the writer, producer and director behind the scenes orchestrating the entire movie? Why, you might ask, would we do this? Why would we ever want to project a scenario where we're being controlled by someone else, especially when people are suffering and dying in the more frightening scenes of our movie? The answer is simple: we put ourself here, smack dab in the middle of all the insanity and suffering, so we would have the perfect environment from which to transcend it all. You see, the outside world is constantly showing us the very issues that we're carrying inside us - the guilt, the judgments, the anger, the impatience, etc. These issues need to be addressed and resolved before we can move on to our highest potential.

From this perspective, we're in school, and the way we graduate is to see everything that seems to be happening around us as a projection that originates from deep within our own mind. It gets really interesting when we realize that we got stuck in our own projection, and that we're here to find our way out. We bought into our own drama, became victims and acted out our parts in the "us vs them" scenes to perfection, not realizing that the world is reflecting our own inner issues back at us. Now, with this realization, we can go back into the projection room, turn the projector off, or change the reels and put on a new movie that has a much happier ending.

People are getting ready to become the Godly Beings that they are.

Part IV
The Ascension Process
Intenders Become Ascenders

The *Intention Process* leads to the *Ascension Process*. This happens automatically when we've manifested most of our desires. We begin to feel happier, lifted up, elevated. There's a lightness in us now that wasn't there before because much of the weighty baggage we've been carrying around with us most of our lives isn't there anymore. It's gone because we intended it. Now we don't have as many attachments holding us to the Earth. We feel like we're ready to lift off.

Non-attachment to things
leads to non-attachment to the body.

This is the position many Intenders are in after practicing the *Intention Process* all these years. We're ready for our next step in life. But what is it? What do we do after we've manifested all the material things we ever wanted? The answer is: we become Ascenders. We begin to look at the bigger picture, and we immediately see so much more than we did before when we were focused on our earthly wants and needs. We're released now to explore our Essence in depth, and we discover that worlds within worlds are right there inside of us. The world we've been attached to is tiny in comparison to the vastness of experiences available to us in the inner realms. The body can be at rest while the mind soars in a limitless playground called Oneness. We're free.

Ascension Reclamation #5

===
I Reclaim my Freedom
I am deliberately fulfilling my desires or letting them go. I maintain my health, my abundance and my peace of mind, no matter what is going on around me. Attached to nothing and no one, and yet playful with everything and everyone, I reclaim my freedom now.
===

Here, then, is a way out for those who feel encumbered by this world. You can manifest enough of your desires and let the others go. This frees your mind from the constant chatter so you can begin to see what it's like when the chatter slows down and comes to a halt. This is how the Ascended Masters do it. They first lighten their load of desires and attachments. They no longer need to want things, build empires, make lots of money, or come together because they're already together. They're already One.

Intenders of the Highest Good
turn into
Ascenders of the Highest Good.

Guidance from a Taoist Immortal

We've had wonderful guidance from the very beginning of the Intenders, namely from our ascended friend, Lee Ching. He has taught us the spiritual side of intending, as well as helping us with any issues that popped up in our daily lives. His gentle advice, always so loving and caring, carried those of us in the original Intenders Circle through many challenges while we worked to integrate these empowering principles into our everyday experiences.

As many of you know from reading my last book, <u>What You Need To Know Now: The Lee Ching Messages</u>, he has had many lifetimes upon this planet, including one as a merciful commander-in-chief of the Lemurian armies. His most recent lifetime was as a Taoist Immortal, having lived well over a hundred years in China.

I remember one of the very first group sessions we had with Lee Ching. There were 9 of us present as Tina said her channeling prayer and closed her eyes. Lee Ching came through so sweetly and told us that he is not embodied on Earth at this time and will not be here again in a body for another century. He spoke briefly about his last lifetime, saying that the Taoist Immortals had a different view of spirituality than many modalities and religions. He said that they believed that God, Atonement, Ascension, Unity, Oneness (or whatever we wanted to call It,) is to be found deep inside us, as opposed to "out there somewhere".

*I'll never forget his next words as he looked straight at me. He said, "Tony, **what you're looking for is what you're looking with.**" To say that I was struck speechless puts it mildly. These simple words had such a profound effect on me, resonating so deeply, that I later ended up making posters around them. I even began my first novel with them. Clearly, they touched something in me that had long been forgotten.*

Your consciousness is immense,
bigger than the sky,
bigger than all of space.
Spend more time looking within
rather than looking without.

The View from the Projection Room

I always liked going to Disneyworld because they had some great rides where I really felt like I was actively involved in the scene. Whether it was Star Wars, where we dropped out into space and proceeded at warp speed, or Honey I Shrunk the Kids, where we felt like we were miniaturized along with the actors, and our seats shook when giant snakes wriggled beneath us - or Soarin, which was my favorite. In Soarin, we were strapped into individual hanging contraptions, hoisted a few feet off of the ground, and, when the lights went out and the images came on the huge screen that wrapped around us, it felt exactly like we were hang gliding over rivers and canyons and beautiful snow-capped peaks. I loved this ride because I knew I couldn't really be hurt.

From a similar point of view, it's the same in real life. Just as a projector sends images through a lens to a giant screen at Disneyworld, so do we project everything we see, hear, smell, taste and feel from our mind outward onto the screen of the world. Only there isn't really a screen; it's all happening in our mind. It's all being projected from deep inside of us.

Now, we know this idea is outrageous for some of you, so let's explore it in greater depth. When we dream at night, we're seeing images and we're actively involved in scenarios of all sorts. We could be being chased by bad guys, or traveling to new places, or meeting the love of our life for coffee. While we're experiencing these scenarios, they seem as real as anything we experience in our daily life. But then, when we wake up, we find that they weren't real at all; they were just dreams that happened in our mind while we were asleep. Could it be that our daily life is a dream, as well, and we're asleep in it, just like we are in our nightly adventures? Could it be that our body is just another image we're seeing along with all the other objects that seem to be outside of us?

What if everything, *including our body,* is just an

image that's part of the projection that's coming from our mind? And what if this image is only a very tiny part of who we really are? If this is so, then when we were little children being taught the ways of the world, we were misinformed about our true identity. We were taught to identify with our body, and this worked fine for us for many years. However, there comes a time in the course of most of our lives when we choose to seek the truth. The great challenge with this is that it typically takes a big shift in our perception in order for us to integrate it into our daily experience. We're asked to become something that we can't see, something deep inside of us, that's capable of projecting entire worlds outward.

Like in the Wizard of Oz, we're called upon to take a look in the projection room and see who is running the whole show. Soon we find out that it's us. I'm running my show and you're running your show - and, like in the Disneyworld rides, we're both sharing the screen. We're both sharing the dream. And we're not identified with our body anymore because we now know that we're projecting it along with everything else we're perceiving.

So, what is this thing that we can truthfully identify with? I call It Essence, but the name most commonly used in our world is "Spirit." Spirit is what we call that which lies deep within us, that which we truly are at our core - and when we actually come in contact with It, *the experience that follows is so grand, so utterly magnificent, that it goes way beyond words, way beyond anything we have ever experienced or ever will experience in our daily lives.* In fact, many teachings refer to this experience as being so sacred that they call it "Holy." They say we meet The Holy Spirit and they tell us that It will teach us anything we ever need to know about worlds within worlds, if we will but let go of our old worldly perceptions and look deep inside ourself.

Ascension Reclamation #6

==
I Reclaim the Atonement
I'm projecting the world I see, like a movie, from deep within my mind. I've been seeing the world as separate images that appear to be outside of me, but now I've shifted my perception inward and I see it all, including my body, as One. I let my worldly projection go and I reclaim the Atonement for myself now.
==

118

The Course

Is there really anything outside of us? *A Course in Miracles* and other non-dualistic teachings would tell us that all of our experiences are happening in the mind, and that there is nothing real going on outside us. It's like when we go to a movie. We sit in the theater and watch the action on a big screen - and we know that what's going on on the screen isn't real. It's just a movie being projected from a booth hidden somewhere behind us. If the flick is enjoyable, we tend to get emotionally involved and forget about everything else for awhile. This is how it is in life. The movie we call "the world" is being projected outward from deep inside us, and we get so involved in it that we forget it's not real. We forget that it's just a movie.

I've taken A Course in Miracles twice and am now taking it again for the third time. When I first took "The Course" in the 1990's I was living outside of Hilo, Hawaii in the rainforest. I had a lot of time on my hands, so it was easy to read the text and do the workbook everyday. I finished it in a little over a year, but, in all honesty, I didn't get it. Even though I resonated with

it, I didn't truly understand or experience what it was
saying.

I took The Course a second time after the turn of
the century when I was traveling to Intenders Circles
around the country. I had extra time for my studies,
in between all the driving, and it took me just under
two years to complete the curriculum. Again, I didn't
really understand the core ideas it was presenting to
me, but something in it was working on me, behind
the scenes of my life.

I started taking The Course for the third time after
visiting with my good friend, Dan Hunter, in Houston
last year. Dan facilitated many spiritual book clubs over
the years, but now he'd stopped reading any books that
weren't related to <u>A Course in Miracles</u>. His favorite
was Gary Renard's <u>Disappearance of the Universe</u>,
which he read along with The Course everyday. I was
staying with Dan for a couple of weeks while I presented
events around Houston, and we would stay up late each
night talking about The Course. To my great fortune,
Dan was able to explain The Course in ways that had
escaped me when I'd read it before. Now it was all
starting to make sense. It said the world isn't real. Much
like a dream, it's a movie I'm projecting from within
my mind in which all things are separated from one

another. There's an experience of being One that I can have once I dismantle the ego that's currently running the projector and keeping the perception of separateness intact. The Course emphasized several times that the experience of Atonement is far more enjoyable than anything the world I'm projecting has to offer. All I need to do is ask the Holy Spirit, or Jesus, or my Inner Teacher for help and I will be helped...

Well, this new way of looking at The Course turned my world upside down. Up until now, I was lost in my own movie. I'd been fixated on the world, using the Intention Process as a path to my Ascension. I knew in my heart that it was working like a charm, but that it would just take me longer. The Course offered a shortcut to the experience I was seeking that uses a new kind of forgiveness.

Once again, both roads lead to the same place. There's absolutely nothing wrong with taking either road. I've been on the path of the world for the majority of my adult life. In fact, it's a good place to start because most of us are already on it (even though some lofty egos might claim otherwise.) Indeed, most folks, myself included, have been working diligently within the world to find something that is not of this world. It's in the projection room. It's in the mind.

The challenge for those who've been stuck in their own movie and are now intending to take a shortcut to get Home is making a smooth transition from one road to the other. That's what *The Ascension Reclamations* are designed for. They're an activational map, a guide inward, for those who are intending to rise up and out of their worldly projection and step into their highest calling.

Like we've said, you can better enjoy the world, with all of its treasures and trimmings, by using the *Intention Process* to help you navigate your way around the mountain. Then, when you've fulfilled enough of your desires, you can leave the world you've been projecting behind and take the *Ascension Process* cutoff that runs straight up the mountain. Both roads lead to the top. Either one will take you Home.

The new awareness comes,
not from the ego,
but from our Higher Self,
The Holy Spirit.

The New Forgiveness

According to The Course, forgiveness is the primary tool for dismantling the ego and awakening us to our highest fulfillment. But it's not talking about the old, typical, run-of-the-mill kind of forgiveness. It's talking about forgiving in an entirely different way. In the old way, we would forgive someone else for doing something we didn't like. Perhaps they scared us, or attacked us, or bruised our ego in some way - and we would forgive them for their wrong-doing. As you can imagine, this practice is full of holes.

First, it declares that something "wrong" was done. As we learned earlier, this is our spin, our ego's judgment, on things: because *nothing is intrinsically wrong with anything.* Einstein told us that it's all relative. One person may see a situation and judge it as being wrong, while another person may see the exact same situation and judge it as the best thing that ever occurred. In truth, the situation just happened, and we need not place any judgmental spin on it. In and of itself, it was neutral, and we could just as easily be grateful for what we learned from it.

Secondly, the old form of forgiveness has an "us and them" factor built in to it. It sees us as the one who has been harmed in some way. And it sees the other person as the bad guy who harmed us. Anyway you look at it, a separation has taken place: the separation between us and the other person. When we begin to look at this through the eyes of the Atonement, we immediately see that there is no us and no them. There is only One of us, and nobody did anything to anyone else. Thus, there's no need to forgive the other person because, when we look at it as One, we're doing it all to ourself.

When seen in this light, the only person we would need to forgive is ourself. However, in accordance with our first parameter for dismantling our ego, namely that nothing is "wrong" with anything, we can entirely overlook the whole situation because nothing wrong was done in the first place. This doesn't mean that we need do nothing when we've falsely perceived a wrong having been perpetrated on us. On the contrary, we need to defuse the emotional charge we've built up from the situation so we can walk away feeling free. And we do this by releasing the original judgment, being grateful for it all and letting it go by turning it all over.

*Lining up with our Higher Self –
that's the next step
for each of us and for all of us.*

Turning It All Over

Like the *Intention Process*, the final step in the *Ascension Process* is letting go - but there's a bit more to it. Just before we let go, we need to turn it over. This means that, other than being open to receive, there is one last thing we can do to insure our success. We can ask for help. We can talk to our Higher Self or The Holy Spirit or Jesus Christ by saying:

Ascension Reclamation #7

==

I Turn It All Over

"Holy Spirit, I turn all of my challenges, problems, issues, desires, dreams, dramas, wants and needs over to you. I know you love me and keep me from harm, and I trust you to watch over me while my prayers and intentions are being manifested. I am grateful to you for all that you do on my behalf. I turn it all over to you now. For the Highest Good of All and Everyone. So be it and so it is."

==

You have help in high places and are wise to call on It as much as you like. BJ used to say, *"You can muddle through your own stuff, or you can ask for help. Muddling takes a lot longer, but help can come in an instant!"*

We know that the idea of your Higher Self or The Holy Spirit being invisible stops many of you at this point. You feel uncomfortable calling on someone or something you can't see with your physical eyes. As with our emotions, thoughts, cellphone waves and the multitude of electronic frequencies that surround us, just because you can't see them doesn't mean they aren't there. In fact, it's not a matter of seeing at all. It's something you feel. As you learn to let go even more, you will become more attuned to what's going on invisibly around you, and you will feel the sweet presence of Your Higher Self come forth when you call.

Not only that, but the proof is in the proverbial pudding. Your success will have manifested. That which you asked for has come to you. More gratitude is in order.

Ask for help from your Higher Self and, step by step, you will be shown.

Coming Home

It's a travesty that our culture supports the idea that when we're done with our body it's the end of us. It isn't true, and yet, there are those who would knowingly hide the real truth from their fellow travelers for the sake of power and money. The real truth is that we go Home. Our focus is returned to the Essence inside us, an Essence that has never left us, but was simply covered over by all the needs of the body. We only need to look a bit deeper to see that this is so.

Obviously, something animates our body. Most people call it Life and presume that it goes away when our body is finished. But just because we're done with our body doesn't mean we're done with the Life that's been living inside it. That Life is simply released to go on to other adventures. Now we're free to bask in the Atonement or to project other worlds that appear to be outside ourself.

It's the world that disappears, not us.
We can't disappear.

We know that the idea of us projecting the world around us is entirely contrary to the mainstream's beliefs around what happens when this world disappears from our view. However, we think it's refreshing, and that, when you fully experience it, you will find it comforting, as well. We've talked about this *"projection"* many times throughout this little handbook, and, as we've said, from our point of view, Ascension is not about flying off to other places in the Universe. It's about first finding out who or what is projecting the movie that we call "our world." It's about finding out who we are. This is our highest priority.

The Hawaiians have an interesting sense of perspective when it comes to losing their loved ones. Instead of saying that someone died or is gone, they say that their loved one just "changed address." They'd say something like, "Oh, brah! I going miss Keala now dat he wen change address!" They don't look at it like their loved one disappeared altogether. The way they see it, their loved one just went somewhere else.

Those who have experienced Life apart from the body will tell you that it's a relief and a release;

that it's to be welcomed, not avoided - in just the same way that Life in the body is to be welcomed, and not avoided. Indeed, Ascenders will tell you that the trick to having this release is to have it while you're still alive. You don't have to wait until you "change address" to experience the wonder and expansion that it brings with it. We can go Home anytime we like without having to permanently lose our body to do it.

It's the lie that's got to die.
The real you cannot die.

Ascension Process Activation

As we said, from our perspective, we do not ascend in the way most people think. The common view of Ascension sees us having a higher experience by lifting up and out of our body and going somewhere out there in the Universe, perhaps to a place we call our home. We then identify with that celestial place and say we're from Venus or the Pleiades, or wherever. People do this all the time.

It's not about meeting a saint or an ET.
It's about having an experience of awakening.

We look at it another way. Since *the extraordinary experience* we seek is to be found deep inside of us - and the world, including our supposed planetary homes, are outside of us - our Ascension is something that proceeds from within. If it were to be happening outside of us, it would just be another projection on our part. In other words, we're projecting the planets and stars, no different than projecting the chair across the room. How can we ascend from a place within the projection? We can't. The only place we can ascend from is our Essence deep inside, and It's always right there with us. We don't need to fly off anywhere to find it.

**When we truly decide to awaken,
it will happen.**

The *Ascension Process* is activated when we reclaim that which is rightfully ours. Our true and real identity, our Oneness with God, has never left us. It's been there all along; it just got lost along the way when we bought into the ideas that we're less than what we truly are, that we're at the mercy of the world around us, and that there is no way out. Now, however, countless millions of us are reaching a pivotal point in our evolution. We're leaving our old ways behind and awakening to our highest potential by using tools like the *Ascension Reclamations.*

In these times of great change, Intenders and Ascenders from all parts of the globe and all walks of life are stepping into the fullness of who we truly are. Amidst powerful adversity, the extraordinary is awakening from long slumber. Hard shells are cracking. Cocoons are breaking open. Spirit is reaching out as we turn inward and *reclaim* our innocence, our perfection, our power, our freedom, our highest vision of ourself...

How silly it was that we thought
we were something less than amazing,
that we were less than immortal.
We've never been less than anything.

The Ascension Reclamations

I Reclaim my Innocence

I've never done anything wrong and neither has anyone else. I forgive myself for thinking otherwise, and I let go of my guilt and self condemnation forever. I reclaim my innocence now.

I Reclaim my Perfection

I am perfect and so is everyone else. I see all of us getting exactly what we most need for our soul's growth in every moment. Everything is right on schedule. No judgments or comparisons are required on my part. I reclaim my perfection and the perfection of all things now.

I Reclaim my Power

The mainstream reality doesn't affect me unless I allow it to do so. I am thinking whatever I want and thus creating whatever I want. By envisioning only positive outcomes, I reclaim my power now.

I Reclaim my True Identity

I am much more than I've been led to believe. No longer identified with my name, my story or my body, I am the Essence embedded within this body. I am Spirit, connected with my Creator forever, unlimited and all knowing, immortal, whole and holy. I am part and parcel of God, and I reclaim my true identity now.

I Reclaim my Freedom

I am deliberately fulfilling my desires or letting them go. I maintain my health, my abundance and my peace of mind, no matter what is going on around me. Attached to nothing and no one, and yet playful with everything and everyone, I reclaim my freedom now.

I Reclaim the Atonement

I'm projecting the world I see, like a movie, from deep within my mind. I've been seeing the world as separate images that appear to be outside of me, but now I've shifted my perception inward and I see it all, including my body, as One. I let my worldly projection go and I reclaim the Atonement for myself now.

I Turn It All Over

"Holy Spirit, I turn all of my challenges, problems, issues, desires, dreams, dramas, wants and needs over to you. I know you love me and keep me from harm, and I trust you to watch over me while my prayers and intentions are being manifested. I am grateful to you for all that you do on my behalf. I turn it all over to you now. For the Highest Good of All and Everyone. So be it and so it is."

To activate the *Ascension Process*, all we have to do is say the seven *Ascension Reclamations* until they become part of us. The *Reclamations* work best when we say them everyday.

Epilogue
Don't Stop Along the Roadside

The view from our land in Kona was breathtaking, spanning the whole southwest coast of the Big Island. Rarely an evening went by without us stopping whatever we were doing to watch the sunset. One evening, just after the sun slipped below the horizon, BJ and I were sitting on a rock wall we'd been working on all afternoon, talking about enlightenment. At that time I hadn't had a glimpse yet, but he'd been enlightened several years earlier.

"What's it like when it happens?" I asked him.

He didn't say anything right away, which was unusual for him. He just sat there gazing out at the ocean. After a moment, he did the strangest thing. He squinted his eyes, almost closing them, raised his brows and lifted his arm up at an angle of about 60 degrees, as if pointing with great devotion toward something that was invisible and slightly out of his reach. I couldn't tell if he was looking at something in the distance or at something up inside his head. "As you keep meditating, Tony, a light will appear between and up behind your eyebrows," he said. "You will know it when you see it.

It will be as if it is calling to you to come to it, but there will also be distractions and the pull of other things tempting you to take detours along the way."

"What kind of other things?" I asked. This was starting to creep me out.

"They can be anything, taking any and every form you can imagine," he said. "And many will do their best to take your energy and keep you from going on to the light. They represent your fears and your unfulfilled desires, and, just like salespeople here on Earth, they can be very alluring and persuasive. Your job, however, is to be brave, keep going, and don't make any stops until you're completely in the light."

He could see that I was a bit spooked by his explanation. Before I could ask anything else, he went on, "You have nothing to worry about, Tony, as long as you keep heading toward the light. Once you're fully ascended into the light, you'll be glad you're there. I've never met one Ascended Master who would trade their experience in the light for anything. Without exception, we're all glad we kept going and didn't stop along the way."

The way out isn't out.
It's within.

About the Intenders

Over the last twenty years, the Intenders of the Highest Good have helped people all over the world integrate the Intention Process into their daily lives, both individually and in community. Embodied in the Intenders information is a call to take our next step in life, and it provides us with the free tools to do it. *The Code, The Bridge, The Intenders Circle, The Law of Agreement, The Vision Alignment Project, The Intention Process* and *The Ascension Process* are all models for uplifting the individual and the group—and, at the same time, lining everyone up with the Highest Good.

A free color poster
of the *Ascension Reclamations* is available at
www.ascenders.org

For more information about the Intenders, visit
www.intenders.com,
www.highestlighthouse.com,
www.visionalignmentproject.com
or www.tonyburroughs.net

About the Author

Tony Burroughs is one of the more prolific visionaries of our time. He is the author of eleven self-empowerment books and the cofounder of the Intenders of the Highest Good community. His widely acclaimed Vision Alignment Project recently surpassed two million alignments. He has produced three full-length DVDs, over 130 YouTube videos for the Intenders Channel and has appeared on numerous TV and radio shows including Coast to Coast AM. Tony lives in Pagosa Springs, Colorado.

Gratitudes

This book exists because we intended it. It was born out of a natural progression that follows when we make conscious intentions and trust that they will manifest for us. In other words, making intentions leads to our Ascension. We didn't know this when we first started out with the Intenders many years ago; we just wanted to create better lives for ourselves and our friends. As it turned out, however, our intention-making led some of us inward and led others to manifesting all sorts of wonderful worldly things for themselves. The thousands of Intenders stories we've received attest to the success they've experienced - and we would like to thank each and every one of them for believing in us and sharing their WINS with us.

The author would also like to express his heartfelt gratitude to several people without whom this book would not have been written. Tina Stober, Betsy Palmer, Vicki Harding and Hazel Martin steadfastly supported this work over the years, encouraging me every step of the way. Anne Whigham, Dean Sanna, Kate Beloved and Diane Leonard read the manuscript and contributed more than they know to the editing of this book. Thank you one and all.

And finally, my gratitude for having BJ and Lee Ching in my life knows no bounds. These loving ascended mentors, with their two distinctly different teaching styles, were always there for me, even when I didn't know it at the time. May they be held in the highest light imaginable.

Resources

If, like many of us, you're enjoying the worldly road and want to use the *Intention Process* to get more proficient at manifesting your dreams and desires, we humbly (and highly) recommend all of the Intenders materials on the next page to you.

While this book, <u>*The Ascenders Handbook,*</u> will guide you inward and introduce you to many of the principles in The Course, it is not meant to be a substitute for The Course. In our experience, there's no other book quite like <u>*A Course in Miracles*</u> for navigating the inward road. If you're interested in taking the *Ascension Process* a step further, we highly recommend <u>*A Course in Miracles.*</u>

FYI: The Course can be a bit overwhelming at first, so, for those of you who would like to jumpstart your journey, some excellent introductory resources are available. <u>A Course in Miracles: The Movie</u> by iKE Allen and Ande Anderson, as well as the works of Gary Renard, Alan Cohen and Michael Mirdad are expressly designed to make it easier for anyone to tap into the core ideas presented in The Course.